THE MOST IMPORTANT SECRETS TO GETTING GREAT RESULTS FROM IT

Everything Your Computer Consultant Never Told You

Dear Lisa,

you have been my inspiration for Marketing — this is for you —

RAJ GOEL

P.S. Don't let Mike Signora :-)

ISBN No: 978-0-9844248-1-8

"Are You Googling Your Privacy Away" was originally published in ISC2's *InfoSecurity Professional* Magazine, Issue #6

"Trends In Financial Crimes" was originally published in ISC2's *InfoSecurity Professional* Magazine, Issue #7

"Power Passwords" appeared in *Entrepreneur* Magazine, March 2011

"Backing Up in the Cloud" was originally published in *Law Technology News*, April 4, 2011. The complete article is copyrighted by John Edwards and Law. com.

"What Should Matrimonial Attorneys Know About Cyberforensics" appeared in the April 2012 issue of the *New York County Lawyers Association (NYCLA)* Newspaper.

ACKNOWLEDGEMENTS

First, and foremost, I would like to thank my wife Sharon, and our beautiful daughters, for putting up with me all these years. Without you, life would have no meaning. You are the reason I get up in the morning, and stay up late at night working :-)

To Crawls & AM—my oldest friends, mentors and role models—a special thank you.

To my mentors at Gotham, BNI and Landmark Education for opening doors, when all I see are walls. Kelly Welles, David Stein, Steve Lichtenstein, Fred Klein, Tom LaCalamita—you know who you are, and what you mean to me.

To Fabian, Arsalan and the rest of my staff at Brainlink—thanks for always making me look good.

To Ilya Zherebetskiy, Mark Bernstein, Mary Twohey—for providing constructive criticism for this book.

To Robin Robins, The Technology Marketing Toolkit team and Tom Malesic of EZSolution—for providing the inspiration and guidance for this book.

To our clients—you honor us by trusting us to manage your networks, take care of your computers, and help you grow your businesses—a heartfelt thank you.

CONTENTS

INTRODUCTION

Who should read this book?

If you are an attorney, accountant, insurance agent, architect or other small business professional with less than 100 employees in New York City, then this book has been written for you. In it you will discover the various options available to help you use technology to run your business more efficiently. You will also find out how to hire an IT firm to enhance your business.

If you're like many business owners, you view technology as an annoying expense, or worse yet, you're still using computers like you did 10 to15 years ago.

But the reality is that computers and technology have grown significantly over the past 15 years. Some of the habits and practices that you learned in college, or when you started your business, are outdated. These are things like defragging, performing backups, and fighting virus infections.

In addition, your job has probably changed from sole employee and Jack-of-all-trades, to owner, chief marketing person and head salesperson.

When you add in sites like LinkedIn, Twitter, Facebook, along with your website, your blog and all the other things needed to grow your business, you'll realize that you too have grown and changed significantly over the past 15 years.

You wouldn't change the oil in your car, perform a root canal or conduct open-heart surgery on yourself, would you? Then why do you or your staff, spend hours each day (or each week) performing your own tech support, installing computers, reinstalling Windows and fighting viruses on your own?

I challenge you to look at your business in a new light.

You and your team are no doubt exceptional at what you do. Your clients choose you, above all others, because you are specialists in your field, and you provide a service or an experience that sets you apart from everyone else.

Brainlink is a team of experienced, customer-focused IT specialists. Founded in 1994, we have extensive experience working with the Financial Planning,

Real Estate, Pharmaceutical and Healthcare markets with a focus on time-sensitive, privacy and/or security oriented solutions.

From 24/7 crisis management, to security analysis and problem solving, we bring a wealth of experience in reducing costs, increasing performance and garnering client satisfaction.

My team can perform the routine work of IT maintenance such as installing or reinstalling Windows, applying patches and updates, setting up and testing backups, maintaining your network, and eliminating spam pop-ups and viruses.

But in addition, we can help you grow your business more effectively by implementing client thank-you campaigns and email drip campaigns. We can also take care of tasks such as converting your pile of business cards into a manageable database, and more.

We have also developed a training video that helps Financial Planners, Accountants and Lawyers get more out of their networking. (This video can be seen at www.businesscardmastery.com). If you'd like to know more about how it's helped our business, and could help yours, don't hesitate to contact me.

Whether you want to spend more time with your family, take more vacations, or simply spend less time in the office while increasing profitability, this book is for you.

Profits increase when costs are lowered, and revenues are increased (or stay the same). Productivity is defined as doing more work in less time, or with fewer resources.

When used properly, a well-maintained network and an updated database can help you reduce your costs, increase your revenues, maximize your productivity, and in turn, increase your profits.

In fact, we guarantee that you will see a 30% increase in productivity over an 18 month period, or you will get your money back. We can confidently make that guarantee because our clients are so satisfied, and profitable, that we've NEVER had to give any money back.

The reason is that over the past 18 years, our clients have consistently increased their revenues, reduced their costs and ultimately, increased their productivity.

WHY DID I WRITE THIS BOOK?

When I meet fellow business owners, the conversation inevitably turns to what they want more of from their business. Many want more revenues, others want more profits, and everyone is convinced that there must be a better way to run their business.

I agree that there is a better way.

Technology is a tool—and most lawyers, accountants, architects, insurance professionals who know their businesses and products exceptionally well, do not understand how to use technology effectively.

When we bring on a new client, the first thing we do is clean up the existing issues.

Problems such as:

- Missing or incomplete documentation—gathering the list of passwords for domain name, e-mail provider, Internet provider, server, etc.

- Missing or incomplete backups

- Outdated antivirus software

- Unpatched machines

I am amazed at how many business owners are willing to put up with:

- Bad service

- IT guys that never show up

- Computer techs who don't know the first thing about running a business—theirs or yours

- Computer personnel who hold their clients' businesses hostage by not documenting, or by changing passwords secretly.

After the first 90 days, I personally spend time with the business owner to understand what makes your business tick. Who are your clients, what do they buy from you, why do they buy from you, and most importantly, how can we boost your billings by increasing your "referability" and improving client follow-ups.

Our clients are amazed and grateful, for the services they receive, and with the responsiveness of my team.

Having consulted with everyone from doctors, to lawyers, to insurance companies, to pharmaceutical companies, to Fortune 100 corporations, what I have learned is that technology is a democratic resource.

The solutions we implemented for Fortune 100 corporations ten years ago cost millions of dollars. These solutions can be implemented today in your business for only a few hundred dollars.

So if you're curious about how technology can improve your business, increase your profitability and elevate your game, or if you're frustrated with your current IT technician or company, then this book is for you.

Message from the Author

My name is Raj Goel. I started Brainlink in 1994, and like most entrepreneurs, I thought that if I simply set up shop, the world would beat a path to my door. And for about 10 years that's exactly what happened. We never marketed, we never advertised, but somehow clients kept finding us and we had more business than we could handle.

But around 2003, something changed. Business dried up. Perhaps it was a combination of the dotcom blowup and 9/11. Or perhaps the world simply changed.

As a result, beginning in 2004, I started networking. I discovered a whole new world of people (amazing people, funny people, generous people) and I learned that as long as I kept networking, and delivering on the promises my business makes, it will keep growing.

I would bet that something similar has occurred (or is occurring) in your business right now. What was once hot and highly profitable can no longer be sold. Through a combination of world events, lawsuits, and new regulations, the operating environment for businesses has changed.

We (you and I) as fellow business owners are all on the same journey. We all want to spend more time with our families, take home more money without working longer hours, spend more time improving our health, getting in shape, and going on vacations. And all of us have reputations worth protecting and a brand worth investing in.

This is My Offer and Promise to You:

Keep doing what you do best—improve the quality of your product, deliver great service, expand your team and refine your expertise.

My team and I will do our best to keep your systems running, lower your costs, and increase your profitability.

CHAPTER 1

THE DOWNSIDE
OF TECHNOLOGY

*"A computer lets you make more mistakes faster than
any invention in human history—with the possible exceptions
of handguns and tequila."*

MITCH RADCLIFFE

In every generation new technology comes about and changes the way we run
our businesses. Initially, it is adopted by large corporations, the super wealthy,
and the trendsetters. Within a matter of years (or these days, weeks) it filters
down to the small business owner, then to the individual.

When the telephone first came out, it was seen as a tool for the industrialists.
No one, not Alexander Bell, not Thomas Edison, nor anyone else predicted or
could have foreseen that today we have anywhere from 1 to 5 phone numbers
attached to us. Our cell phone, the office phone number, our home phone
number, the fax line, the Google voice/follow me anywhere number, etc.

In the 1950s, AT&T put ads in their phone books to educate large business
owners on the value of 800 phone numbers. Back then an 800 phone number
cost you several thousand dollars a year.

Today you can buy a personalized 800 (or 877 or 888) phone number for as
little as $15 a month. All of a sudden, you have the same capabilities today
(in fact, better capabilities) that the largest corporations did just 20 years ago.

Similarly, when the IBM PC came out, it too was marketed to large
corporations. Most small business owners could not afford the $5,000 or
$10,000 price tag. Today the cheapest cell phone you can buy has more
horsepower than the first-generation of PCs.

Today, even the smallest of businesses, is asked (required?) to produce compelling visuals, good looking websites, killer PowerPoint slides, blog posts, e-mail and print newsletters, etc.

This is the true downside of technology—things you never thought you'd have to do in your business or things you thought were reserved for the Fortune 500 are now required of your business.

The other downside to technology, of course, is that it breaks down—often at the worst time possible and in the most inconvenient way. Whether it's your car breaking down on the side of a highway in the middle of nowhere, your cell phone losing battery far away from the charger, your e-mail being inundated with spam, pop-ups everywhere, or your computer running really, really slowly, these are problems that we have all experienced from time to time.

Individually, these are all nuisances. If you're a single person or a solo-preneur, they can be annoying. But if you're a business owner, these nuisances can quickly become very, very expensive.

For example, let's say you're an attorney who bills at $200 an hour and a computer is down for four hours. You have potentially lost $800. Not a small sum, but not a huge sum either.

If you're the senior partner in a law firm with 20 employees and your e-mail server goes down and your gross billings are $10,000 an hour for the entire firm, then you just lost $40,000. That is a large sum of money.

You may be old enough (and wise enough), to work without your computer and/or cell phone. After all, agents created insurance policies using nothing more than pencil and a calculator for decades; lawyers have been creating briefs with nothing more than pen and paper for centuries; and architects have been drawing blueprints with pencil, paper and rulers for centuries.

But can you say the same for your staff? The 20-year-olds and the 30-year-olds who've never lived a day without e-mail, instant messenger, Skype, Facebook, Google, Wikipedia? Does your staff even know what a printed encyclopedia looks like? Probably not.

This is where we come in.

We ensure that your machines are updated, with no viruses or Trojans roaming your network, and that your backups are up-to-date.

Most importantly, we give your staff our phone numbers and our e-mail addresses. So when they have a problem or a question, they can bother us, not you.

You deal with the clients—whether it's reviewing proposals, selling policies, taking them out to golf or simply holding their hand.

Let us deal with your staff—including their computer problems and computer usage issues. We will also train them on how to use their tools better.

COMPUTER CONSULTANT HORROR STORIES

No book on computer consulting would be complete without horror stories. Some of you may be reading this book simply for the horror stories, and others unfortunately, are living these horror stories.

If any of these stories are familiar to you, please feel free to call me, or drop me an e-mail.

Unlike most licensed professions, there are no licensing standards or credentialing bodies for the IT consulting industry. That means anyone, anywhere in the world, can declare themselves a computer consultant. Most business owners have no way of verifying whether the consultant is really an expert in the field, or whether they are completely incompetent.

Without further ado, I present to you some classic horror stories we've encountered over the years:

A financial planning client had a really good IT guy who built and ran their systems well. Then he disappeared—literally. About six months later they found out that he had left the state and gotten a day job in a different field. The client was left with outdated backups, incomplete passwords and no documentation. Luckily, nothing had crashed, and we were able to reset passwords, proactively update systems, test backups, etc.

Another firm had been working with an IT guy for 15 years. A good guy—not great, but okay. The IT guy suffered a heart attack and his doctor told him to take it easy. As a result, he started scaling back his services. Initially, the client (like all human beings), empathized with *the IT guy and let him recover his health. What they didn't realize is that when the server crashed a year later, they had no backups and no documentation. Recovering the server, reclaiming their domain name and fixing their e-mails cost about $30,000. More importantly, it took them over six months to recover.*

Another client worked with a very well-known IT consulting company. They were on the classic hourly billing/time-and-materials agreement. This is also known as the taxi meter agreement—the IT guys get paid by the hour so they have no interest in getting it done faster or cheaper. As a client put it, he was afraid to call the IT guys because he wasn't sure whether it was a two-minute thing or a two hour thing. But he knew, that every phone call or e-mail for tech support resulted in a very expensive bill. If you feel that your IT guy is running a taxi business, give me a call.

More and more, I'm meeting business owners whose IT guy (or company) hasn't seen them in over a year.

This is not uncommon for people of our age.

Unless there is a major health concern (like when a friend has a heart attack or is involved in an accident), we see our doctors once a year, maybe.

And while the dentist requests that we schedule an appointment every six months like clockwork, the reality is that most of us go once a year, if we're lucky.

Car dealers would love for us to come in every 3,000 to 5,000 miles for servicing. And some of us do that religiously. Most, on the other hand, only go to the mechanic when trouble lights appear on the dashboard or funny noises start coming from the car.

Computers, however, are a different beast.

Unlike our bodies, they fail faster. Computers require constant upkeep and maintenance.

A good IT company (like ours), can maintain your systems 24/7 remotely without running up your bill.

You don't have to remember to schedule appointments, or take a computer to the shop. We can log in remotely and work on them during evenings and weekends or come on-site, as needed.

I am not going to delve much further into horror stories—you know better than I what a bad computer consultant has cost you in lost time, lost revenues, and lots of stress.

I'd rather focus on how we can improve your productivity and profitability.

Chapter 2

How Much Is Lost Productivity Costing Me?

The productivity of work is not the responsibility of the worker, but of the manager.

PETER DRUCKER

Whenever we talk about investing in technology, most business owners ask, "what is it going to cost me?"

They almost never ask, "what's the cost of not doing it" or "how can I become more profitable?"

Most business owners (and their accountants) do not compute the value of intangible benefits.

If you've ever bought a car, had a great meal, or watched a really good movie then you know that the cost and benefits isn't a simple matter of dollars and cents.

The car that you love does more than take you from point A to point B—it gives you freedom, it gives flexibility of travel, it gives you your private space to think, and in some cases sing out loud to songs you haven't heard in 20 years (or the ones your kids think are corny).

We can compare the dollar-cost of car ownership to the cost of taxis, trains and other means of transportation.

Similarly, a great meal—whether it's in a five-star restaurant or your favorite hole-in-the-wall, has benefits beyond simply providing you food and nutrition. It makes you happy and fills you with a satisfaction that can last for days or even weeks.

Think about these two examples for a minute—we can calculate the cost of buying or leasing a new car, car insurance, gas, parking, etc. We can also calculate the cost of food, travel time, etc.

However, nowhere on your balance sheet or P&L statement will you find a line item for calculating the value of the joy of driving or the joy of the great meal.

Your accountant may not be able to tell you how much downtime cost your business this year or how much you've spent on lost productivity. You, however know at a gut level that every crash, every virus, every pop-up and every computer upgrade ever done, has cost you far more than dollars and cents.

We call these "productivity losses" or "lost opportunity costs".

Here are some ways your company is losing productivity and lowering your profits:

1. If your staff or receptionists are performing calculations on a calculator and then typing them into Excel because they don't know that Excel can calculate sums, averages, totals, subtotals, sort and organize data, then your staff is doing more make-work than real work.

2. If you spend more than 10 seconds looking for an e-mail or an attachment, or worse, you can't find the e-mails or attachments and have to ask people to resend them, then you are suffering from productivity loss.

3. If the appearance of your proposals, presentations, reports or PowerPoint presentations hasn't changed in years while your competition's materials look snazzy, then you are hobbled in the marketplace.

4. If you've ever experienced spam, pop-up or viruses then you already know how irritating that can be. Worse yet is when slow or infected computers degrade your staff's faith in your systems. If they cannot trust your systems, then they will spend more time doing defensive work—copying files to external drives or USB drives, storing e-mails in multiple locations, uploading your documents to the "cloud," or finding other ways to ensure data is not lost. Unfortunately, these measures waste time and cost you money.

5. If all of your contacts and calendars are not easily accessible and synchronized between your desktop, smart phone, iPad, etc. then you are in danger of losing thousands of dollars in lost business each month. It's not uncommon for you to meet people and set up appointments only to have to reschedule them, often at the last possible moment. Can you do that easily? Can you juggle appointments between your work computer, home computer, cellphone or tablet?

6. Finally, if you're a smart business owner then you are already networking. The Chamber of Commerce, BNI, Gotham Networking, attorney/accountant roundtables, industry conferences, and more.

Are you getting value for your time and energy?

Do you have a system in place that scans and organizes each business card that you receive, that tracks when and where you met people, that makes information available to you and your team in Outlook Express, your smart phone, and your CRM (if you have one)?

If not, then what was the point of going to that networking event? **The reality is that most networking groups follow the 90/10 principle**. 90% of the people go to the meetings and complain that they're not making any money. **10% of the people go to the same meetings, have great follow-up systems and make 90% of the money.**

Which group would you like to be in?

A good computer consultant is more than just a mechanic or technician who fixes your computer. He or she is an information management expert (and fellow business owner) who can help you use information systems wisely, to grow your business more effectively.

The first question you should ask your computer consultant, or anyone pitching for your business, is "how are you going to help me grow my business this year?"

Here are some ways we help our clients grow their businesses:

1. By eliminating (or minimizing), spam e-mails, pop-ups, and viruses, we reduce downtime.

2. By implementing proper backups, better e-mail solutions, and faster computers, we help your staff do more work in less time

3. We observe how your staff uses their systems, and where appropriate, we work with them to better utilize technology. It could be something as simple as having a complete signature at the bottom of each of their e-mails, or something as powerful as teaching them how to create visually compelling, beautiful to look at, effective presentations.

4. Working with you, the business owner, or your sales/marketing person, we put together a business card contact management database. We use a card scanner to scan the cards, but then we go beyond that. We train you (or your staff) on how to properly organize these cards and how to integrate them into a unified marketing system.

   This allows you maintain contact with your clients, prospects and centers-of-influence, with e-mail, post cards, greeting cards, birthday cards and gifts, and do it on a consistent regular basis, throughout the year.

5. Poor salespeople spend 90% of their time chasing new customers. Smart salespeople, and business owners, spent 70% of their time getting more business and referrals from existing customers. Whether you got a customer two years ago, 10 years ago, or 30 years ago, chances are they don't really know all the services that you provide. We can help you engage with your clients better.

For example:

Insurance Agents/Brokers—If a client bought a life insurance policy from you, do they realize that you also sell long-term care or disability or business buyout policies?

Attorneys—If you were hired to complete a real estate closing or incorporation documents, are your clients aware that you also provide Trust & Estate planning, bankruptcy and other services?

Architects—If you have been hired to design their house, or add an extension, does this client know that you can also assist them with alterations and repairs or fixing code violations? Have you let them know that you have a large list of qualified, certified, reliable contractors, other tradesmen and realtors that they can work with?

CPAs—When you started out, all you may have done was their annual taxes. Today, you provide tax minimization guidance, wealth preservation strategies, bookkeeping services, and other services that your clients aren't buying from you—yet.

In each of these cases, we've helped our clients put together consistent, automated, low-cost, highly effective marketing and follow-up systems that have helped them:

- Get more business from existing clients
- Get referrals from existing clients
- Get introductions from existing clients
- Get new business from people they've met in networking groups, social gatherings, etc.

CHAPTER 3

WHAT ARE YOUR OPTIONS FOR IT SUPPORT?

"If you think it's expensive to hire a professional to do the job, wait until you hire an amateur."

—RED ADAIR

OPTION 1: DO IT YOURSELF

Either you, or a member of your staff who may be very expensive and better utilized elsewhere, is trying to do a technician's job. How is that working out for you? Chances are— not very well.

At worst, it creates gross inefficiencies in your network. At best, it is not going to be as efficient or as effective, as getting the job done by an experienced IT professional.At worst, it creates gross inefficiencies in your network. At best, it is not going to be as efficient or as effective, as getting the job done by an experienced IT professional.

OPTION 2: USE A NEIGHBOR, FRIEND, COUSIN, NEPHEW, ETC.

We are all neighbors, friends, or relatives to someone else. And where possible, and appropriate, it's nice to be able to help out someone like that. The question you have to deal with is whether this person has the skills, the mentality and the experience to manage systems and grow your business. Or are they better utilized elsewhere?

OPTION 3: USE SOMEONE WHO DOES IT ON THE SIDE, AFTER HOURS OR ON WEEKENDS

Just like doctors who moonlight, or bookkeepers who do taxes on the side, the quality and reliability of these people can vary. Some are absolutely fantastic; responsive and knowledgeable about what they're doing. You should be grateful, and thank them.

Many however, are amateurs. They have a day job doing something else, or working for someone else. This is a hobby for them. They don't run a business, and in many cases, never have and never will.

OPTION 4: OUTSOURCE IT TO A TEAM OF EXPERTS

Would your clients hire you if you were only doing the job as a hobby?

Would you like your cardiac surgeon to be someone who performs heart transplants and stent implantations regularly, or someone who dabbles in it on the side for extra money?

If you demand that your cardiac surgeon be the best in his field, then shouldn't you demand that the heart of your company (the network, servers, computers, e-mail and databases) be taken care of by an expert?

Chapter 4

Paying for IT

"There ain't no such thing as a free lunch (TANSTAAFL)."
—ROBERT HEINLEIN

Whatever you have (and whatever you get) is going to cost you—now or later.

Hourly Support

This is the classic IT billing model. When you're starting out this makes the most sense. You don't have a lot of money, you don't have a lot of needs and quite frankly you're probably still trying to figure out what your business is.

As your business grows however, this becomes a significant expense.

Look around your business. At one point you probably did all the check writing, bookkeeping and accounting. Today though, you may have a CPA who does your taxes quarterly. And you probably have a bookkeeper or someone similar who does the data entry, balances your checkbook, and gives you and your CPA, information at a lower cost.

The same is true with IT. If you're starting out as a 1 to 2 person shop, then by all means, use the hourly model. But if your company has more than five people or is more than five years old, then you really should look for a more appropriate business relationship.

Limited Remote Support

There's a new breed of companies who offer limited remote support at very low price points. These are the companies you see advertising on late-night TV or at trade shows, where they offer to support your business at $39 per computer or some other lowball rate.

But be aware before signing on that a lot of these agreements have a number of gotchas or "out of scope" services. For instance, these companies may monitor your computers and may even apply patches or updates remotely. But anything other services will cost you plenty. And these companies have a huge menu of à la carte services that you may need at some point.

I'm not saying these companies are bad. However you should read the contract carefully. These companies are the McDonalds of IT support. Their staff tends to have low levels of training, so they cannot handle complex or complicated problems. Due to inadequate training, they may sell you incorrect or inadequate products. But most importantly, they may have no legal or contractual liability if they botch things up.

MANAGED SUPPORT PLANS (MSP)

A managed support plan (MSP) is what we offer at Brainlink. For a flat fee every month, we provide the services your business needs to grow and prosper. These services include things like patches, updates, virus removals, backups, upgrades, training, and more.

We also provide on-site and remote support. If we can't fix a problem remotely, we will show up on site, without charging you travel or hourly fees.

More importantly, we will be in your offices on a monthly basis (if not more often), so that we can understand the culture of your business and observe the day-to-day on goings of your company. We can then provide appropriate tools, training, and recommendations to make your staff more productive.

This may be as simple as giving everyone in your company (with your approval) remote access via LogMeIn and setting up your iPad with remote access, or as complex as showing your staff how to turn your existing proposals and reports into killer documents.

Yes, I have a vested interest in recommending a managed support plan. And yes, I am biased in favor of a managed support plan.

Why?

Because, as a business owner, it aligns your interests with mine.

I'm an entrepreneur, just like you. I want to make as much money as possible and the best way for me to do that is for **you to have as few problems as possible**.

You too are an entrepreneur, just like me. You too want to make as much money as possible. The best way for you to make as much money as possible, is to sell more to your clients, to make more profit per product or project, and to spend less time fighting your computers.

Doesn't that sound like a confluence of interests?

We both have an aligned interest in running your business better, giving you less downtime, and making your business more productive and more profitable.

Chapter 5

Questions To Ask Your Current IT Consultant

How you do ANYTHING is how you do EVERYTHING.

HARV ECKERT

BUSINESS QUESTIONS:

1. **Do they have a written and guaranteed response time for your calls?**

   Does your computer consultant guarantee to have a technician working on your problem within a specific time period after receiving your call or e-mail? If they don't guarantee a certain response time, then be prepared to work within their time frames and not yours when a problem does arise.

   A written guaranteed response time should be standard in every service agreement you sign. After all, it's no good to get great service if you have to wait three days for it.

2. **Do they explain what they are doing and answer your questions in terms that you can understand (not geek-speak)?**

   Communication is a part of every business, and every relationship. Most divorces start because the couples are no longer communicating effectively, or at all. Most clients drop their vendors because of a communication gap or misunderstanding.

   Does your IT consultant speak to you in plain English, to ensure that you understand what's being done, why it's being done, and how it will help your interests? Or are they just throwing jargon and meaningless buzzwords at you?

There are no stupid questions and there are no stupid clients—only impatient technicians who don't want to take the time to explain.

Good technologists are educators by nature and training. It's not enough to just fix the problem; we also take the time to understand why the problem occurred and how we can prevent it going forward.

And for that, we need your team's cooperation and trust.

We earn your team's trust by working side-by-side with them, taking time to understand what they do, and what's important to them. We talk with your staff, not talk down to them.

We KNOW that they are doing their best to deliver the best service they can, and OUR job is to help them do it better.

3. **Have they provided you with written network documentation detailing what software licenses you have, critical network passwords, and hardware information, or are they the only person with the "keys to the kingdom?"**

    We meet a lot of business owners and office managers who have no idea what their server passwords are, or where the domain name registration info, service contract and warranty information is.

    Every business should have consistent, updated documentation detailing a list of all the vendors, contract numbers, warranty expiration dates, passwords, network design diagrams and other information that's critical to keeping the business running.

    If your IT guy is the only person with this information and you have a sneaking suspicion that he's using this knowledge as a means of holding your business hostage, or for job security, then get rid of him immediately. This is unethical, dangerous to your organization, and could create legal liability for your business. So, don't tolerate it!

4. **Do they have adequate errors and omissions insurance as well as adequate workers compensation insurance to protect YOU?**

    Your doctor has malpractice insurance. Your lawyer has malpractice insurance. Your architect and engineers are personally liable if they provide incompetent service.

Does your IT guy have errors and omissions (E&O), cyber liability and workers compensation insurance to protect you?

Everyone makes mistakes—that's human nature.

But if your IT guy's mistake costs you several days of downtime, or hundreds of thousands of dollars in losses, why should you pay for it?

In this litigious society you better make sure that whoever you hire is adequately insured for E&O, cyber liability and workers compensation insurance—and don't be shy about asking them for proof of insurance.

5. **Will they provide references and testimonials?**

A good company should have a long list of current, glowing testimonials and references. More importantly, you should be able to contact the references whenever you like. Don't just take the sales guy's word for it or believe their website—testimonials can be faked or be really out of date.

Before hiring, ask the IT company for references in your industry, and then call these references. Ask them what they like and don't like about the IT company.

Hiring an IT company is no different than hiring an employee, or finding a good lawyer, CPA or adviser. Ask your friends, check their references and follow your gut.

6. **Do they provide detailed invoices that clearly explain what you are paying for?**

Don't you hate it when companies send you an invoice and you have no idea what it's for? Does your IT company give you clearly detailed invoices? Do you understand what you're being charged for, and do you agree with the charges?

If not, ask for clarification. Or select a vendor who bills in English.

7. **Do they complete projects on time and on budget, or does every project end up taking longer and costing more than you expected?**

There are very few things your business will do that will be new, unique or never dealt with before. The reality is, you are probably not running a cutting-edge business, so you shouldn't be on the bleeding-edge of technology.

Therefore, done properly, scheduled upgrades and projects shouldn't go beyond your time and dollar budget. Ask your IT company for their track record on projects and upgrades. Or better yet, look at their bills to you. If they're coming in on time and budget, congratulations.

Otherwise, you might want to reevaluate your working relationship.

8. **Do they offer any guarantees on their services?**

   Guarantees should be more than boilerplate text—they are a promise to you, your staff, and your clients. Ask your IT vendor what guarantees they make about their competency, their experience and most of all, their results.

   We guarantee a 30% decrease in downtime, and a 30% increase in productivity over 18 months.

9. **Do they arrive on time and dress professionally?**

   You have a dress code, and a standard for your staff. It may be blue jeans and denim shirts, or three-piece suits from Brooks Brothers.

   Does your IT firm's staff match (or exceed) the visual presentation that you expect of your staff? Or are you embarrassed to have technicians working in your office when an important client is present?

10. **Do you have to manage their progress on projects, or do they provide frequent updates, status reports, and follow-up calls and e-mails?**

    Professional IT firms should provide constant and thorough updates on open items, current projects and known issues. Just as your clients expect you to keep them updated about their projects and tasks, your IT firm should keep you updated about the state of your technology, open projects and requests.

    One of the things our clients rave about is our responsiveness to client inquiries, updates on projects, and overall communication with you—our clients.

11. **Do they consistently (and proactively) offer new ways to improve your network's performance, or do they wait until you have a problem to make recommendations?**

Your computer consultant should routinely sit down with you and discuss ways to improve your business. And not every solution should require you to spend more money.

We show our clients how to lower their costs and increase efficiencies. We share techniques/technologies that are working in our business. Our goal is to help you become happier, more profitable and less stressed.

Does your IT company do that?

TECHNICAL QUESTIONS:

12. **Are they remotely monitoring your network 24/7/365 to keep critical security settings, virus definitions, and security patches up to date?**

A remote network monitoring system watches over your network 24/7, keeping an eye on your router, firewalls, exchange databases, the health of your servers, the health of your desktops, the condition of your backups and a whole host of other, critical information required to keep the business running.

In short, the network monitoring system catches problems BEFORE they turn into bigger problems or cause downtime.

13. **Do they have other technicians on staff familiar with your network in case your regular technician goes on vacation or gets sick?**

It's a fact of life that people get sick, people go on vacation, and people change jobs. Can your computer consultant (or his team) step in and manage your technology when your regular technician is sick or on vacation?

14. **Do their technicians maintain current certifications and participate in ongoing training, or do you feel as though they are learning on your dime?**

Every year doctors, lawyers, CPAs, architects and other professionals are required to get CLE's/CPE's to maintain their professional certifications and credentials. Your computer consultant should be no different.

Are they constantly growing their skills and honing their expertise, or are they selling you outdated practices, procedures and advice?

BACKUPS AND DISASTER RECOVERY

15. **Do they INSIST on maintaining an offsite as well as an onsite backup, or are they letting you rely on outdated tape backups?**

Is your IT consultant still using tapes?

8-track is dead. CDs killed the audiotape. So are you still using tapes to back up your business?

Hard drives are thousands of times faster than tapes, much more reliable, and less expensive to maintain and support.

16. **Do they INSIST on doing periodic test restores of your backups to make sure the data is not corrupt and could be restored in the event of a disaster?**

A backup is only as good as the last restore. If you can't recover data when it's needed, then the backup is useless.

We have seen a number of companies that thought they had good backups when in reality the backups are corrupted, software outdated or simply, not running.

Your computer consultant should be performing a monthly test of your backups, and confirming that the data and settings can be restored in the event of an emergency.

17. **Do they offer flat-rate or fixed-fee project quotes, or do they give themselves a wide-open playing field with "time and materials?"**

If you've ever hired an attorney on an hourly basis, or simply taken a ride in a taxi, then you know how painful it is to get billed by the minute or by the hour. A good computer consultant should not only advise you on the right technology and tools required to grow your business, but they should also do it at a flat rate or on a fixed fee basis.

Never let a computer consultant or anyone else try to put you on a "time and materials" basis.

INFORMATION SECURITY COMPLIANCE

18. **Is your computer consultant knowledgeable about HIPAA, PCI, GLBA, FMLA, etc. and how other consumer protection/privacy laws apply to your business?**

I don't have a problem with globalization, if you don't have a problem with globalization.

However, if you are an insurance professional, a medical professional, an accountant or a lawyer, then state or federal laws (such as HIPAA, GLBA, RED FLAG, Privacy Breach and others) may prevent you from using vendors located overseas. The reality is that most other countries do not have the same regulatory or legal framework as the United States.

I have delivered over 3,000 CLE/CPE hours across the USA to attorneys and accountants in New York, New Jersey, Pennsylvania, Delaware, Texas, Illinois and California.

That's not a claim most IT consultants can make.

Nor can they claim to have written articles in major information security magazines about Compliance, Trends in Financial Crimes, or Protecting Your Kids From Social Media.

Remember, if (or when) you get sued, ignorance of the law is NOT a valid defense.

CHAPTER 6

COMMON PITFALLS AND
WORKING WITH COMPUTER
CONSULTANTS

The difference between genius and stupidity is that Genius has limits.
ALBERT EINSTEIN

As human beings, we are trained from birth to trust the experts. Whether it's your parents, teachers at school, professors at college, or doctors and lawyers. While your computer consultant is an expert, he or she is not perfect. They're human, just like you and me.

DON'T BLAME THE COMPUTER CONSULTANT

Yes, even with the best support your computer or network may have problems. Machines die, hardware fails, software has bugs. Don't automatically assume this is the computer tech's fault.

Work with them to get the problem resolved in a rapid, cost-effective manner.

If you keep experiencing the same problems over and over again, then perhaps it IS the computer technician's fault but usually it's more complicated than that.

It could be that your systems are 5, 6, or even 10 years old, and need to be upgraded or replaced. Some IT consultants are hesitant to recommend upgrades, and some business owners fear having this conversation, because all they see are the potential costs—and none of the benefits. Before we perform an upgrade, we will discuss with you the pros and cons of upgrading, and where possible, demonstrate the key benefits well before you approve the upgrade.

It could also be that some of your staff visit dangerous sites, or perform activities that compromise network security or system stability.

In any case, we will take the time to fix the problem, understand why it occurred, and then communicate the recommended approach to resolving the issue permanently.

PROTECT YOURSELF FROM MALWARE, VIRUSES AND SPAM

No amount of technology and tools can protect you from human error. And while there are some viruses and Trojans that can get in undetected, most of the time, they are let in by your employees, or yourself.

Five years ago, when the computer got infected, the question we used to ask is "where were you shopping" or "what porn sites were you looking at?"

Since 2009, whenever we see an infected computer the first question we ask is "what were you doing on Facebook?"

If your business does not depend on Facebook or YouTube to get new clients (and I assert that most professional businesses—i.e. lawyers/doctors/CPAs/ architects do not get business from Facebook, YouTube or the Internet) then it's better to block these sites or limit access to them.

We have seen more businesses get infected by new staff "Facebooking" during business hours or surfing sports sites during the Super Bowl, World Series, or other sports events than any other method—combined.

We will work with you to develop good, practical, useful computer security policies and procedures. At the end of the day however, it is your business and you have to set the standard. Most employees are busy doing their jobs— some however, seem to treat the office as an extension of their home or social life. These employees need to be educated, properly trained or terminated.

THE TRUTH ABOUT COMPUTER SECURITY AND COMMON SENSE

The truth is, for every company that is attacked by sophisticated hackers, there are hundreds more that get broken into because they fail to take basic precautions.

Precautions such as:

- Updating their computers on a weekly or monthly basis.

34

- Applying security patches and upgrades when warranted.

- Changing passwords on a regular basis, at minimum every year.

- And the number one reason that companies are broken into is: their staff use the same password everywhere.

Think about this for a minute—these shouldn't be earth shattering revelations. However, on a daily basis we meet business owners and companies who haven't applied patches and updates in months or even years. They have the same antivirus software that came with the machine years ago, and it's expired. Or worse, the anti-virus software that came with the computer is inadequate.

- Will we recommend good, industrial grade firewalls? **Absolutely.**

- Will we recommend that you and your staff use strong passwords? **Yes.**

- Will we train you and your staff in creating strong passwords? **Yes.**

- And most importantly, will we help protect your systems by updating and patching them regularly? **Absolutely, undeniably yes.**

THE BIGGEST THREATS TO YOUR SECURITY AND PROFITABILITY

The biggest threats to your security and profitability are your newest employees, your interns and those employees who think they know more than the computer technicians.

Most college students, interns and new employees have never grown up in a culture of privacy.

They don't think before tweeting about your newest client, problem at work, or other issues.

They don't think before posting office gossip, sensitive information, and other things on Facebook or LinkedIn.

In many cases, we've seen 20-somethings spend hours each day tagging photos on Facebook, posting updates, and otherwise wasting time.

Not only do these activities waste time, and cost you money, but they can also lead to infections, and public disclosures of otherwise private data.

In my experience, the biggest threats to your business are your new employees, disgruntled employees, government and regulators, and lastly hackers.

We can't do much against a determined hacker—no one can.

We can help you build the proper policies, procedures and practices to comply with laws and get the government regulators (and compliance officers) off your back.

Most importantly, we can work with you to teach your employees that "loose lips sink ships".

With your approval, we can provide written materials, flyers, one-on-one training and seminars on social media security, Internet best practices, and an overview on information security/consumer privacy laws and regulations that apply to your business.

CHAPTER 7

GETTING THE MOST OUT OF YOUR COMPUTER CONSULTANT

In the land of the blind, the one-eyed man is king.

DESIDERIUS ERASMUS

Now that you know what questions you should ask your computer consultant, and how to find honest ones, let's take a look at how you can get the most of your relationship with them.

A good computer consultant will let you concentrate on your business—whether that's designing buildings, selling insurance, drafting contracts or protecting your clients in litigation, or management real estate portfolio. Let him or her worry about the backups, keeping out viruses, spam, and pop-ups.

A good client/computer consultant relationship is no different than a doctor/patient or business owner/CPA relationship. You don't have to know the intricacies of what your doctor does or the nuances of tax laws that your CPA does, but you do have to ask them the right questions, and trust their answers.

Here's how you can use technology, and your computer consultant, to grow your business.

1. **Have a regular meeting** (whether it's monthly or quarterly) with your consultant.

2. **Ask about the state of your business**, any problems they are encountering or concerns they have. You should also request additional resources/coaching/training as needed for employees.

3. **Share with your computer consultant your business challenges**— whether it's pending terminations, client difficulties, or your own frustrations in dealing with computers at work or at home.

4. **Treat your computer techs the way you want to be treated.** Yes, you are paying the bills and you are the client. But your computer consultant (and other vendors) are also professionals, and in some cases, fellow business owners. Creating an adversarial relationship helps no one.

5. **Ask what upgrades or technology could benefit your business.** You don't have to agree with every recommendation, or sign off on every upgrade. However, if you have this open dialogue, then you might see things that could benefit your business.

6. **Ask your consultant how other clients of theirs** (in your industry and other industries), **are doing.** What are their challenges, what solutions are they using and could any of these solutions benefit you.

7. **Ask your computer consultant for referrals and introductions** to potential clients, employees and centers of influence.

CHAPTER 8

360° PROTECTION

Home computers are being called upon to perform
many new functions, including the consumption
of homework formerly eaten by the dog.

DOUG LARSON

As a business owner, you have to be able to work from anywhere and everywhere—home, office, airport, beach, hotel, etc.

For most business owners, working from home has become a mandatory reality. If that's true for you, then have your office IT consultant setup the systems in your home office correctly.

At minimum, have them check the following:

- Is your anti-virus and security software up to date?
- Can they remote into your home computers?
- Are patches and upgrades being applied?
- Is your Wi-Fi secure?
- Does your home network have multiple security zones—to isolate your computer from your kids and spouse?
- Is your home router or firewall appropriate for your needs?
- Can you VPN or remotely connect to your office?
- Does your iTunes, AppleTV or home digital-entertainment system work properly?
- Can you work (or play) from your iPad, iPhone and other devices?
- Can you print to your home printer and/or the office printers?
- Are your work laptops/desktops isolated from your kids and spouse? This is highly important in the event you enter into divorce

proceedings against your spouse, or if your business gets sued by an ex-employee, client, vendor or competitor.

- Are your employees home computers secure?

- Or are you letting your most valuable people jeopardize your company?

CHAPTER 9

INFORMATION SECURITY POLICIES AND EMPLOYMENT AGREEMENTS

To err is human—and to blame it on a computer is even more so.

ROBERT ORBEN

A common mistake I see small business owners make, is that they do NOT plan for lawsuits. In our litigious society, the question isn't "Will I get sued," but **"When will I get sued?"**

While no Information Security Policy or Employee handbook can protect you from lawsuits, proactive planning can minimize your litigation costs, consultant costs and opportunity costs.

COMPONENTS OF A GOOD INFORMATION SECURITY POLICY

Depending on your business, and applicable State and Federal Laws, your policies should contain the following:

1. **Which laws or regulations this policy addresses** (e.g. HIPAA, RED FLAG, HIPAA/HITECH, etc).

   a. Remember to update the policies annually, or as the laws and enforcement changes.

2. Any technical or specific requirements the law specifies

   a. **PCI compliance requires**

      i. **setting minimum password lengths,**

      ii. **how often passwords must be changed,**

41

       iii. **how often security patches must be applied,**

       iv. **What types of encryption is allowed, etc**

  b. **HIPAA/HITECH requires** that

       i. **your backups must be tested regularly,**

       ii. **you must have a written, and tested Disaster Recovery Plan.**

  c. **State Privacy Breach** laws (depending on your state) may require you to

       i. **Notify affected clients in writing**

       ii. **Establish an ombudsman or designate a specific individual to handle all incoming client inquiries**

       iii. **Nofity the State Attorney General's Office**

       iv. **Etc.**

3. Notify your staff that everything done on the company premises, or using company equipment is subject to the company's security policies

  a. Everything they do online can be monitored by the IT team or the Security Compliance Office

  b. All emails, documents, ideas, etc are property of the company

  c. If employees access their personal Email, Facebook or other accounts using company equipment, then these can be seized by the company during a **litigation hold** or pending litigation.

4. Establish your policies and procedures that allow employees to let the IT guys and/or their manager know about problems, breaches, and other issues without recrimination.

  a. People ARE going to make mistake.

  b. Someone WILL click on a popup that infects the company

  c. Someone WILL accidentally delete critical files or emails

  d. Someone will look at porn, conduct illegal activities or otherwise expose your firm to harassment or bias lawsuits.

e. Your staff WILL know when a database is getting corrupt, or a system is failing.

f. In any of these cases, they should have the ability to notify the IT team, their manager or legal counsel (as appropriate) without the fear of termination

You should know what a litigation hold is—

- How it impacts what you can and cannot do with your office computers, your home systems

- What your employees can and cannot do with their home systems

Between HIPAA/HITECH, PCI-DSS, GLBA and State Privacy Breach laws, chances are that you are already **required** to have these policies in place.

If you haven't already done so, start putting them in place now.

If you haven't had your (at minimum) annual security training seminar for your staff, schedule it asap.

As always, if you need help in putting these together, call me at 917-685-7731 or email me at raj@brainlink.com.

Please note: I am not an attorney, and this is not legal advice. If you have a good tech-savvy attorney, use them. If not, contact me and I can introduce you to attorneys who draft these policies constantly.

CHAPTER 10

INCREASING PROFITS AND PRODUCTIVITY

It is not about bits, bytes and protocols,
but profits, losses and margins.

LOU GERSTNER

Here are a few ways to increase your profits and productivity.

1. **Give yourself and your staff dual monitors**. Studies show that large monitors and dual monitors can increase staff productivity from 20% to 40%.

2. **Upgrade any computers that are more than 3 years old**. Since computers double in speed and power every 18 months, a three-year-old computer is at minimum 1/4th (and in many cases 1/16th) as fast as a new system. You are doing more with your computers today than you did three years ago—sending and receiving more and bigger e-mails with larger attachments, creating bigger PDF files and larger PowerPoint presentations. If your computer is too slow to handle all this, it's time to upgrade. Your time is far too valuable, and far too expensive to be wasted waiting on a slow machine.

3. **Synchronize your contacts and calendars** across your desktop, laptop, cellphone, home computer and tablet. It surprises me that people either still rely on cables, or don't sync their data across their devices, at all.

4. **Setup a company-wide Wiki or knowledgebase**. A wiki or knowledgebase allows your staff to share knowledge, intelligently. Whether it's a NEW CLIENT INTAKE process, SEMINAR PLANNING requirements, or simply steps to book your next flight,

anything that your staff does on a regular basis should be documented in a wiki or knowledgebase.

5. **Upgrade to Windows 7 and Outlook 2010**. If you are an avid Outlook user and you are continually searching for e-mails or attachments, then Outlook 2010 is quite simply the most important upgrade you can make. Your computer can search through 1 million e-mails and find the ones you are looking for in less than a second. Think about it—searching your e-mails and getting results as fast as searching the internet with Google!

6. **Upgrade to Word 2010**. The new templates and styles features of Word 2010 turns boring old documents into gorgeous, stunning, well-designed documents. It may sound superficial, but looks do matter. And a better looking proposal or report will get a much better reception than an old style document.

7. **Increase your Internet speed**. Very often, we find that the number one complaint from your staff is that the Internet is too slow. And yes, five or seven years ago high-speed Internet was very expensive. Today, you can have 10/20/50Mb of Internet speeds for a few hundred dollars per month. This simple upgrade alone can have a phenomenal impact on your staff's productivity.

8. **Invest in a business card scanner**. If you are a confirmed networker than you probably have a large stack of business cards on your desk (or you soon will). Business cards sitting on a desk, stuck away in a drawer, or lying in a pile are useless. Worse, they are a waste of the time you devoted to you took to attend the event,and the money you spent paying for it. We can train you, and your staff, to scan and organize business cards correctly, and convert new contacts and prospects into clients.

9. **Exercise more**. Why is your computer consultant telling you to exercise more? Because your body is the most powerful tool you'll ever have. And your health is the most valuable asset you will ever have. Invest in both—exercise, eat right (when you can), and sleep better.

10. **Play more. Play with your kids**, your grandkids and your spouse. Very few people get up every day and go to work to make more money just for the sake of making more money. We are good at what

we do and we like doing it professionally. But we're really doing it for our families. Let's not forget that—our kids won't stay little forever. Pretty soon they'll be in high school or college and starting families of their own. **Spend time with them. Now.**

11. **Take more—and longer vacations.** Studies show that regular vacations recharge your mental and emotional batteries, make you happier and your business more productive. Whether it's a weekend of golf, a week in the Bahamas, or a month-long cruise in the Mediterranean just do it. The business will run without you. Your clients will survive without you. And when you come back, you'll see your business, your staff and profit opportunities in a whole new light.

12. **Read "The 4-Hour Workweek" and "Get Things Done".** These two books belong on your reading shelf. Better yet, they belong inside your brain, and your teams' brain. Read them, give them to your staff and your clients. Both of these books contain an amazing amount of practical tips and techniques for delegating, increasing productivity, increasing efficiency and living the life you've always wanted. Yes, the title of the 4-hour workweek is hokey and I haven't quite gotten there myself. However, I have gone from working 160-hour weeks to working 60-hour weeks, while doubling profitability.

13. **Speak and present in public.** You are an expert in some area of your business or industry. While there might be 1000 insurance agents around you, and 200 other attorneys in your line of business and 50 architects within 1 mile of you, chances are you do something that no one else does. It could be the niche market that you service, or interesting materials that you work with, or interesting cases that you been involved in, or simply a hobby that is unique or highly popular. Malcolm Forbes, the publisher of *Forbes* magazine is quite popular and famous for riding his motorcycle and his hot air balloon. Neither of these were directly related to his business, but they certainly made him memorable.

14. **Implement a structured marketing campaign.** Any modern business needs to stay in touch with their clients, contacts, prospects, referrals, reporters and industry thought leaders. We help you create multi-touch campaigns that lets you:

a. Follow-up with new contacts and networking colleagues via e-mail

b. Send postcards, gift cards, birthday cards and thank you gifts to clients

c. Send "thank you for that referral" gifts to your referral sources

d. We help you send out print/e-mail newsletters to clients, prospects and thought leaders (no, we aren't web or print designers…but we can use yours, or recommend some good ones who can create the templates. Once we have good templates, we can help you use them to communicate with your clients and prospects more effectively).

e. We implement the technology, provide the tools and the training you and your staff need to market and grow your business.

CHAPTER 11

GROWING YOUR
SOCIAL CAPITAL

The Time is NOW and the person is YOU.

NIDO QUEBIEN

1. **Practice being a CONNECTOR, not just a networker.**

    a. Have you read an article that's related to a client, prospect or friend's business? Email them the URL or paragraph.

    b. If you see a request like "I need..." or "I want to meet..." or "XYZ is looking for a job in...", make a connection.

2. **Keep your LinkedIn Profile Updated**

    a. Update your SUMMARY section so it's more conversational

    b. Remove old/useless recommendations

    c. Link to articles you've written, been quoted in, or find interesting

3. **Keep your website updated with news stories, articles you've written, etc.**

4. **Volunteer to speak at events**

5. **Use HARO (Help A Reporter) to get quoted in newspapers, magazines, TV, etc.**

6. **Make time every week to NETWORK, not just show up at meetings**

7. **Meet with people BETWEEN meetings**

8. **Invite people to Coffee, Drinks, Lunch, etc.**

9. **Send people Greeting Cards, Brownies, Chocolate, etc. out of the blue**. But do NOT send stuff on major holidays (4th of July, Memorial Day, etc)—everyone else does that.

10. **Send 1-2 funny/humorous emails a year that set you apart.**

CHAPTER 12

USE LINKEDIN AS A COMPETITIVE INTELLIGENCE TOOL

The difference between a $1 bill and a $100 bill is the MESSAGE written on the paper.

JOE POLISH

Very often, business owners ask "**How can I grow my business in this economy**"? **The most common answer is, networking**. Business Chambers, BNI, Gotham, Trade conferences, various societies, alumni groups, etc.

Many marketers will tell you **ADVERTISE**, use Social Networking—Facebook, Google+, Twitter, Pinterest, etc. as a component of your outbound marketing activity (e.g. spams your friends, family and strangers you met at the last cocktail party…)

For most white-collar businesses (Accountants, Lawyers, Architects, Insurance Agents), there are legal or social norms as to why they can't advertise or solicit as easily as Real Estate brokers, Soda makers, Car manufacturers, etc.

Frankly, if a white collar business got 500 new clients in 6 months, they might go under from the overload. Most professional firms require 1-10 new clients a month. Don't believe me? Check your sales records. How many new clients did you get last month? Last quarter? Last year? Chances are, you have a long, soft-touch sales cycle.

There's an old adage that says "Salespeople spent 90% of their time chasing new customers. **Smart salespeople spend 50% of their time getting more business from existing customers.**"

So, how do you grow your business smartly? Datamining! Or as we used to call it, competitive intelligence.

Keep tabs on what your

- Clients are up to—what new initiatives they're up to? Who are they connecting with?

- Business connections—who they know? What they're working on, etc.

- Find new employees or business partners

- Research the people you'll meet at the next trade show or conference

Here's a PDF tutorial on using **LinkedIn as a competitive research tool** at http://www.brainlink.com/whitepapers/2009-03-23-RajGoel_Growing_Your_Business_Using_LinkedIN.pdf

CHAPTER 13

THE TRUTH BEHIND INTERNET SECURITY

I don't have to outrun the bear, I just have to outrun the competiton.
ANONYMOUS

How effective are Internet security tools these days and what new tools or processes should I be using to protect electronic access to my business records and communications?

The first thing to note is that talking about Internet security by itself makes no sense. That's akin to asking, "How do I protect my car in the garage?" without looking at the overall security of your house, neighborhood and locality.

When people talk about Internet security, what they really mean is, "**How do I protect my sensitive information?**"

Information security involves:

Determining what and where are your information assets—databases, paper files, online systems, emails, accounting systems, PDAs, laptops, etcetera;

Classifying the assets by value; Determining who should and should not have access to that information;

Determining which regulations and standards apply to your business. At the federal level, Gramm-Leach Bliley, HIPAA and Sarbanes-Oxley provide written standards that organizations must meet, depending on the nature of their business or clientele. At the state level, 46 states have passed State Privacy Breach laws (California's SB-1386 was the first, while New York and Massachusetts have the toughest). So if you have clients in any of those 46+ states, complying with those laws is a must.

At an industry level, one standard stand out: PCI-DSS for any company that accepts credit cards, regardless of industry.

PCI-DSS is an industry standard, and does not have the force of law behind it. However, complying with it can improve business practices, provide competitive advantages and even provide a safe-harbor defense in case of a breach.

Putting systems in place to enforce security, log unauthorized access, etcetera.

Thus, there is no simple answer to information security–each organization is different, as is how they conduct business and the culture of each firm will determine the choice of tools and success of the individual information security program.

In my experience, a good InfoSec program requires the organization to become aware of existing laws and how they impact the organization.

E.G. Gramm-Leach-Bliley, for instance, expanded the definition of financial institutions to include real estate firms, auto dealerships and appraisers. So if you appraise property, hold funds in escrow or otherwise lend credit in the course of doing business, GLBA may consider you a financial institution and requires that you safeguard clients' personal identifiable information. Failure to secure PII can results in penalties including civil monetary fines of varying amounts as high as $1 million or more, prison sentences of as much as five years, lower examination ratings and increased reporting requirements, and enforcement actions, which can include board resolutions, memorandums of understanding, written agreements and cease and desist orders.

A good InfoSec assessment answers the following questions:

- What business are we in?
- Where do our clients come from?
- Who are ARE our key clients?
- Which clients or lines of business should we get rid of, outsource or spin off?

Complying with the laws and standards helps your company stand out from its peers, reduces liabilities and damages in case of breaches and increases profitability.

In my experience, one of the things we uncover is the roadblocks and logjams that are interfering with productivity: e.g., If the way forms are handled or cases are approved (or projects are delivered or goods are sold) is too slow or too cumbersome. This is usually the case when the process or service was built 10 or 20 years ago.

In many cases, we reduce transaction time, increase deal flow and/or reduce staff and labor costs by analyzing the information flows, diagramming the information-flow touch points and working with our clients to eliminate roadblocks.

When fixing the issues ("remediating the gaps" in InfoSec jargon), new technology and faster systems can be brought in that really show results at the bottom line.

I worked with a large retailer to complete a **PCI compliance assessment**, and shaving 1/100th of a second per transaction (multiplied by millions of transactions per month) **led to a significant increase in profits.**

For a **health care chain**, the result of the **HIPAA compliance** efforts was the adoption of a new electronic health record system that reduced errors, eliminated patients filling out the same medical intake questionnaire again and again, reduced keying and transcription costs and led to better health care.

Reduced waiting times also allowed the medical offices to book more appointments.

For a **commercial property management firm**, we identified systems and services that were being hosted by third-party vendors that were bleeding the business. We moved these critical systems in house and **saved the client a fortune.** Moving them in house also led to lowered compliance and management costs.

So, what's your information security policy?

What business practices and roadblocks have you been tolerating that, when removed, could increase your profits by 10 to 30 percent?

CHAPTER 14

WHAT ARE SOME GOOD SECURITY DEFENSE PRACTICES?

I have an affection for a great city. I feel safe in the neighborhood of man, and enjoy the sweet security of the streets.

LONGFELLOW

Information security is a lot like the common cold—statistically, everyone catches the cold. Some people avoid it for years, while others get it yearly, and every year a surprisingly large number of people die from untreated colds and seasonal flus. A breach or break-in is a question of when, not if. You will be broken into, you will get infected—the only questions are when it will happen and whether you'll be able to deal with the infection. Now, let's look at some good information security defense practices.

GOOD SECURITY CONSISTS OF USING SEVERAL TOOLS TO DO THE JOB PROPERLY

Use a good spam firewall or service to prevent junk from getting into your mail servers, desktops, et cetera.

Use a good UTMS (Unified Threat Management System) to automatically scan network traffic (both inbound and outbound) for infected packets. Deny malicious packets from entering your network, and investigate all PCs, laptops, et cetera that originate garbage from your network. After all, you do not want the rest of your company's email to be affected, or to have your Internet connection terminated because your network is accused of spamming the Internet.

Use good, managed switches, firewalls and routers. Switches come in two varieties: managed and unmanaged. Unmanaged, or dumb, switches are what you get at your local megamart. They're cheap, and, like your first car, will do a decent job of moving traffic from one device to another.

Managed, or smart, switches, on the other hand, are not usually sold at your local big-box retailer (they're available online at PCMall.com, CDW.com, NewEgg.com and Amazon.com). They cost a bit more, but can give your network abilities you never knew you needed. Capabilities include VLANS (which split one physical switch into multiple, isolated virtual switches), logging traffic and analyzing traffic.

And then there is anti-virus software.

Most desktop-based anti-virus software is junk.

According to av-comparitives.org, an independent lab that tests all major anti-virus/anti-spyware tools regularly, even the best tool has a 69 percent success rate. So if you used the latest product and configured it properly, there's a good chance almost a third (31 percent) of the malware could still come in. Thus, you still need to use an AV/AS product, and we recommend using multiple tools simultaneously–or switching to Macs or Linux and ditching windows completely.

Furthermore, it would be wise not to put all your eggs in one basket. For decades, the military has successfully used the concept of network isolation. Everyone has two or more workstations, one for general purposes (in the corporate sector these might include emails, Web surfing and proposal writing) and one for sensitive purposes(such as financial planning, budgeting, accounting and R&D).

In the consumer space, we tend to use our PCs for everything from video games to solitaire to online banking to emails and shopping.

Imagine living in a one-room house that combines the kitchen, bathroom, bedroom, living room and dining room.

Not very appetizing, is it?

Now apply that to your PC or laptop:

Start separating higher-value or highly sensitive activities from general-purpose activities.

PCs are cheap.

Using a KVM, or virtual machine, you can give people access to classified resources without compromising security.

Finally, when and where possible, look at alternative operating systems and browsers.

Replace Internet Explorer and Safari with Firefox, Opera or Chrome.

Disable/uninstall Outlook Express, and use Outlook2010 or webmail for email.

If you must use Windows (and yes, we live on Exchange, Outlook, Quickbooks, et cetera), then consider virtualizing it.

There are huge benefits to a properly virtualized server and desktop farm. We've reduced help desk and desktop support costs by 50 to 90 percent by moving to VMs.

Remember: The best defense is defense in depth.

CHAPTER 15

WHAT DOES 2012/2013 HOLD FOR LARGE MEDICAL PRACTICES AND HOSPITAL HIPAA/HITECH COMPLIANCE?

Health is the greatest gift, contentment the greatest wealth,
faithfulness the best relationship.

BUDDHA

For many medium-to-large healthcare organizations, the default answer is "**more of the same**". That's also the **wrong answer**. Here's why.

In November 2011:

- NIST released the **HIPAA Security Rule toolkit**

- The Joint Commission (JCAHO) issued guidance stating **health care professionals should not use text messaging for orders**

- US Department of Health and Human Services (HHS) released updated HIPAA enforcement highlights

In 2011:

- UCLA Health System, Cignet and Mass General paid sizeable, and precedent setting penalties.

- HHS conducted joint raids with FTC, State Attorney Generals and US Postal Service Inspectors that led to scores of arrests.

- The HHS **wall of shame** grew significantly larger.

In 2011, Brainlink:

- Conducted an in-depth **HIPAA compliance audit** for a major **RHIO**

- **Assisted several IT firms** in conducting IT Security and Compliance audits for their clients

- **Educated several thousand** CISSPs in **Privacy and Security challenges with Cloud Computing**

- Provided **Ethics CLE** and **CPE** training to several hundred **attorneys and accountants**

If you haven't had an **HIPAA Security Rule mandated Information Security Compliance Audit** within the past 24 months, let's talk.

If you have questions about what your **employees, contractors and Business Associates** can and cannot do, with patient data, let's talk.

If you have questions about HIPAA, PCI-DSS, GLBA, RED FLAG or other compliance issues, call me at 917-685-7731 or email raj@brainlink.com.

If you want to really grow your business in this economy, let's meet.

CHAPTER 16

WHAT DO SMALL MEDICAL PRACTICES NEED TO KNOW ABOUT HIPAA AND HITECH COMPLIANCE IN 2012?

It is health that is real wealth and not pieces of gold and silver.

GANDHI

Do you still think HIPAA compliance is strictly for the big guys?

Do you still think your small medical practice or medical billing business is safe from hackers, criminals and litigators?

From the March 12, 2012 *NY Times*:

> **The New Year's Eve burglary of a California office building has led to the collapse of a national medical records firm.**
>
> *Impairment Resources LLC filed for bankruptcy Friday after the break-in at its San Diego headquarters led to the electronic escape of detailed medical information for roughly 14,000 people, according to papers filed in U.S. Bankruptcy Court in Wilmington, Del. That information included patient addresses, social security numbers and medical diagnoses.*
>
> *Police never caught the criminals, and company executives were required by law to report the breach to state attorneys general and the Department of Labor's Office of Inspector General. Some of those agencies, including the Department of Labor, are still investigating the matter, the company said in court papers.*
>
> *http://blogs.wsj.com/bankruptcy/2012/03/12/burglary-triggers-medical-records-firm%E2%80%99s-collapse/*

Is YOUR practice encrypting hard drives and flash drives embedded within Laptops, Desktops, Servers, Copiers, Voicemail systems and other smart devices?

Within the past 12 months, Brainlink:

- Conducted an in-depth **HIPAA compliance audit** for a major **RHIO**
- **Assisted several IT firms** in conducting **HIPAA Security Compliance audits** for their clients
- **Educated several thousand** CISSPs in **Privacy and Security challenges with Cloud Computing for Healthcare Institutions**

If you haven't had an **HIPAA Security Rule mandated Information Security Compliance Audit** within the past 24 months, let's talk.

If you have questions about what your **employees, contractors** and **Business Associates** can and cannot do, with patient data, let's talk.

If you have questions about HIPAA, PCI-DSS, GLBA, RED FLAG or other compliance issues, call me at 917-685-7731 or email raj@brainlink.com.

If you want to really grow your medical practice in this economy, let's meet.

CHAPTER 17

IS YOUR REAL ESTATE BROKERAGE MAKING THE SAME MISTAKES AS CORCORAN?

Success is a choice. Winning is a habit.

ANONYMOUS

Historically, businesses have assumed that all data generated by their employees or contractors, and/or stored in their paper or digital files and computers belongs to the business. This has been the legal standard in the United States for more than 100 years, and for most industries, this is still the correct position to take.

But not if you are a real estate brokerage. Not in New York State.

Why?

In 2002, Corcoran fired one of their top agents and then denied this agent access to her client list. Like most businesses, Corcoran claimed it was their property.

In 2009, the New York State Supreme Court disagreed, and **awarded the former agent $400,000 in compensatory damages.** Because real estate agents are usually 1099 contractors, not W2 employees, the court stated that **the list is "the property of the agents, not the company".**

Has your Employee Handbook been updated to address this issue? Or is it still providing outdated and legally incorrect advice?

Does your **Employee Handbook** and **Client Privacy Training** take into account the rules and constraints that **Gramm-Leach Bliley (GLBA), FMLA** and the **Patriot Act** impose on your business?

Or are you letting your 1099 contractors and employees land you in potential legal hot water?

If you haven't had an **Information Security Compliance Audit** within the past 24 months, let's talk.

If you have questions about what your employees can and cannot do on your computers, with your data, let's talk.

If you have questions about HIPAA, PCI-DSS, GLBA, RED FLAG or other compliance issues, call me at 917-685-7731 or email raj@brainlink.com.

If you want to really grow your business in this economy, let's meet.

CHAPTER 18

PLANNING YOUR NEXT OFFICE MOVE

Luck is when preparation meets opportunity.

SENECA

Inevitably, at some point, you'll have to move your office. Here are a few tips for making your next move less stressful.

1. **4 months before the move**, as you look at office spaces with your Real Estate Broker, have your IT professional review the space as well.

    a. The IT professional should contact the telecommunications providers and determine what types of internet connectivity and voice options are available in the desired space.

    b. It's NOT enough to simply check out the building. In many buildings, the floor you rent space on, can impact your internet and voice bill dramatically. Here's a dramatic example.

        i. **In a well-known Class A building in Manhattan, floors 1-38 were well connected with low-cost, high-speed cable available. But on floors 39 and 40, no such facilities existed. The cost difference to have the same speed internet circuit between Floor 38 and Floor 40 was $3,500 per month!**

    c. Once a space has been selected, and before you sign the lease, confirm that the internet carriers you want, at the speeds you need, are available in the space you're considering.

2. **90 days before the move**, order the desired internet and voice services in the new space. Have them install the circuits at least two weeks prior to your move-in date.

3. **60 days before the move**, ensure that YOU have all your passwords for servers, desktops, domain name servers, domain name registrars, backup servers, etc.

4. Order a router, firewall, switch and backup server for the new space

   a. **30 days before the move**—Have your IT professional TEST all the backups, and confirm they are reliable.

   b. Contact reliable, building-approved movers and plan the move

      i. **Lay out the floor plans for each employee, filing cabinets, etc.**

      ii. **If possible, try to move into your new offices on a Thursday evening**

5. **14 days before the move**—Configure the router, firewall and backup server in the new space

6. **7 days before the move**—Replicate your encrypted backups into the new space

   a. Monitor the internet circuits in the new space for speed, reliability and performance characteristics

7. **Moving Day**

   a. Enable the MX backup features on your spam filter service, so all emails are stored online, instead of getting bounced or rejected

   b. Update DNS records to reflect the IP addresses in the new space

   c. Let the movers pack and move the computers, furniture, etc.

   d. Order pizzas, coffee, etc for your employees and the movers (nothing breeds loyalty and greater effort than free food!)

8. **The Day After**—While your staff sets up their physical environment (cubicles, offices, artwork, etc), the IT team should be dealing with the digital infrastructure

   a. Setup the server (s)

   b. Re-enable email delivery

   c. Reconnect the desktops, fax machines, copiers/scanners

   d. Update the documentation!

Chapter 19

Is Cloud Computing Appropriate For Your Practice?

I mean if you put all of your eggs in one basket, boy, and that thing blows up you've got a real problem.

JERRY BRUCKHEIMER

What is Cloud Computing?

Simply put, Cloud Computing is a new name for shared computing. In the old days, companies used to rent time on big, expensive mainframes. Then PCs were invented and we started doing most of our work on them. With the rise of the internet, people realized that some problems required massive data centers, and thousands of computers. Google, Gmail, Facebook, Twitter, and Amazon are all examples of cloud computing vendors and services.

Should you use Cloud Computing?

The answer depends on:

- Who you are
- What your business does
- What agreements you have in place with existing clients and vendors
- What federal and state laws apply to your business

If you're in a non-regulated, non-compliance oriented business (e.g. Florists, Restaurants, Caterers, etc) then moving your email to Gmail or Intermedia and your documents to Google Apps makes financial sense.

LEGAL THREATS IN USING CLOUD COMPUTING

ECPA—1986:

The Electronic Communications Privacy Act of 1986 was passed when Reagan was president; the IBM 386 was the most powerful PC you could buy; CompuServe was the internet and Prodigy was email.

ECPA did not foresee Gmail, Hotmail, Facebook, SalesForce.com or any cloud technologies.

ECPA is still the law of the land, and here's what you should know about it:

Summary of ECPA:

1. Any emails held on a 3rd party provider have 180 days of 4th amendment protection. After 180 days, the Federal Government considers them abandoned.

2. Any information stored in an online database had 0 days of 4th amendment protections.

According to EPIC.org—http://epic.org/privacy/ecpa/

Whereas an email stored on a home computer would be fully protected by the 4th Amendment warrant requirement, an email stored on a remote, cloud computing server may not be. More and more information, including documents, emails, pictures, personal calendars, and locational data is being stored in the cloud. Many of these types of information are offered little or no protection under current law. Protections for locational data, in particular, have been widely discussed, but, to date, have not been added.

The 180 day distinction within ECPA is also the subject of much criticism. When ECPA was passed in 1986, web-based e-mail, such as Gmail, did not exist. Instead, e-mail primarily existed in local intranets where clients would download their messages from the server and the server would, generally, not keep a backup. Congress presumed that any e-mails left on the server for more than 180 days were effectively abandoned. This distinction, however, is no longer as relevant today.

According to the ACLU (http://www.aclu.org/technology-and-liberty/ modernizing-electronic-communications-privacy-act-ecpa), PrivacyRights. org, etc.

"The outdated Electronic Communications Privacy Act (ECPA) is allowing the government to engage in a shopping spree in the treasure trove of information about

who you are, where you go, and what you do, that is being collected by cell phone providers, search engines, social networking sites, and other websites every day."

Patriot Act, 2001

Passed in the aftermath of the 9/11 attacks, the PATRIOT act made it much easier to conduct surveillance on Americans.

From Harvard University http://cyber.law.harvard.edu/privacy/Introduction to Module V.htm

A 'sneak and peek' warrant is one in which the government obtains a warrant and executes it without providing notice, or providing a delayed notice to the target.

The Patriot Act creates broad exceptions to the rule that notice must be given in a timely fashion. [...] law enforcement must only show that the investigation will be jeopardized by giving notice. **Under this low standard, it is easy for law enforcement to conduct searches without giving timely notice to the party being searched.** *Execution of this sort of 'sneak and peek' search warrant greatly increases the chances that the search will be performed without supervision and will result in an unnecessary invasion of privacy. This section does not contain a sunset provision.*

What this means to you, in plain language, is that your vendors (Verizon, AT&T, ISPs, webhosts, Google, Microsoft, SalesForce.com, LinkedIn.com, etc.) must give the US Government copies of your data, without notifying you.

As a law-abiding citizen, I don't have a problem with that. I assume that you don't either.

As a business owner, however, I have serious problems with ECPA and the PATRIOT ACT. ECPA and PATRIOT acts are in direct conflict with my legal responsibilities to my clients under HIPAA, GLBA, and State Privacy breach laws. Here's why:

Example 1:

Let's assume you are subject to HIPAA, GLBA, NASD or other privacy law compliance, and your vendor is forced to give a copy of your data to the government.

Somewhere down the road, that data becomes public through a data breach on the government's side, a FOIA request or mishandling by the cloud vendors.

What do you think your clients will assume?

Will they assume that you lost their data, and this constitutes a privacy breach, thereby opening you up to civil and criminal lawsuits?

Or will they understand that the data leak was outside your hands?

Example 2:

Again, let's assume you are subject to any of the 5 Federal Data Privacy laws and/or 43 State Privacy Breach laws and your cloud vendor gets broken into.

What happens to you?

A) Your clients can sue you for a privacy breach.

B) Your State's attorney general and/or the local DA's office can sue you for a privacy breach.

You, as the custodian of PHI or PII are legally liable for it's security.

Are your vendors liable?

If you pay them, then all you have is a commercial contract. Your only remedy is a breach-of-contract lawsuit. If you use free or freemium services, then you have no contract and the liability is fully yours.

LISTEN TO WHAT MICROSOFT AND GOOGLE HAVE TO SAY ABOUT THE PATRIOT ACT:

Microsoft:

"Can Microsoft guarantee that EU-stored data, held in EU based datacenters, will not leave the European Economic Area under any circumstances—even under a request by the Patriot Act?"

*Gordon Frazer, managing director of Microsoft UK, explained that, as Microsoft is a U.S.-headquartered company, it has to comply with local laws. Though he said that "customers would be informed wherever possible", **he could not provide a guarantee that they would be informed—if a gagging order, injunction or U.S. National Security Letter permits it.***

*He said: **"Microsoft cannot provide those guarantees. Neither can any other company."***

While it has been suspected for some time, this is the first time Microsoft, or any other company, has given this answer.

Any data which is housed, stored or processed by a company, which is a U.S. based company or is wholly owned by a U.S. parent company, is vulnerable to interception and inspection by U.S. authorities.

ZDnet, June 28, 2011, http://www.zdnet.com/blog/igeneration/microsoft-admits-patriot-act-can-access-eu-based-cloud-data/11225

Google:

[Sergey Brin, Google Co-founder] acknowledged that some people were anxious about the amount of their data that was now in the reach of US authorities because it sits on Google's servers. He said the company was periodically forced to hand over data and sometimes prevented by legal restrictions from even notifying users that it had done so.

The Guardian, April 15, 2012 http://www.guardian.co.uk/technology/2012/apr/15/web-freedom-threat-google-brin

IS THE CLOUD APPROPRIATE FOR YOUR PRACTICE?

If you are an Attorney, attorney-client privilege conventions, and state privacy breach laws may inhibit your ability to use cloud vendors.

If you are an accountant, state privacy breach laws, and ethical guidelines from your local Society of CPAs may prevent you from using the cloud.

Doctors, Pharmacists, Radiology labs, and others involved in healthcare should be especially careful, as HIPAA and HITECH regulations put the burden of compliance, and protecting patient privacy on YOU, not on your vendors.

If you're a financial planner or Insurance agent/broker, you need to check with your compliance officer(s) or your home office. NASD regulations, the Gramm-Leach-Bliley Act, HIPAA and HITECH compliance rules and the policies of your carriers may prevent you from using the cloud.

In all these cases, the worst case scenario is if your company moves to the cloud, and then finds out, months or years later, that this was a legally indefensible move.

Moving AWAY from the Cloud:

1. The county of Los Angeles spent 2 years and millions of dollars planning their move from an internally-hosted email system to Google's gmail. A few weeks before the final move, the FBI prevented the LAPD from moving to Gmail, due to security policies and agreements that the LAPD had signed with the FBI, decades ago. See http://safegov.org/2011/12/15/los-angeles-pulling-the-plug-on-gmail-at-lapd-is-much-bigger-than-you-think and http://www.pcmag.com/article2/0,2817,2367023,00.asp.

2. United Kingdom defense contractor BAE Systems planned to adopt **Microsoft's** Office 365 cloud-based productivity platform, but was warned against it by their lawyers. Though BAE Systems would be operating outside the U.S., Microsoft's headquarters are in the U.S., and the company is subject to U.S. laws. http://wallstcheatsheet.com/breaking-news/patriot-act-threatens-american-cloud-computing.html/

So, if you're an attorney who handles matrimonial cases, check with the guidelines from the Family law committee of your state bar. If you're primarily a Bankruptcy, Real Estate or Debt Collection attorney, then check agreements with existing clients, as well as GLBA requirements.

Please note: I am not an attorney, and none of this should be construed as legal advice.

I strongly recommens that before you move to the cloud, you should conduct due diligence.

Do your existing contracts allow you to use cloud vendors?

Do your industry guidelines or federal laws permit you to use the cloud? And will it make financial sense for you to do so?

Does the Cloud make Financial Sense?

The cloud is sold as a cheaper option. And in the right circumstances, it can be.

Think of the cloud as a hotel. If you need to stay in LA or Chicago for a few days, staying at a hotel is much cheaper than renting an apartment or buying a house.

However, if you plan to stay for a few months, renting an apartment might be cheaper.

If you plan to stay for years, then buying a house is cheaper, and has significant tax advantages.

In practical terms, if you're a small startup company, or you can't predict your computer usage (one day, you have a thousand visitors, and the next day 10 million), then using the cloud makes sense.

A few years ago, the New York Times wanted to digitize and convert all their issues and images into digital formats. Using in-house resources, this would have taken decades. By using the cloud, they were able to finish the project in a few months.

For most small businesses however, our client base doesn't grow from 1000 to 1,000,000 overnight. Nor do we need to process millions (or billions) of documents. In these cases, using an in-house Exchange server, or an internal fileserver makes much more sense.

This isn't to say that the cloud has no place in your business. Your website, your blog, and your wiki can stay in the cloud.

Your financial applications, files, emails, client documents and other sensitive information, should probably stay in-house.

When in doubt:

- Read your Security Policy (if you have one)
- Check any agreements you signed with your key clients
- Look at existing state and Federal laws, as they apply to your industry
- Check with your attorney
- Contact an information-security expert

Chapter 20

What Are Other Business Owners Saying About Brainlink?

"When a technology problem comes up that no other technology consultant can solve, I call Brainlink"

Brainlink's staff always finds a solution and gets the issue resolved without taking much more of my time then the time it took to pick up the phone or send a quick email. That allows my office to focus on growing our businesses, championing progressive public policy, and fighting for what's right. We are able to take care of our core missions while they worry about the technology, so we don't have to."

Benjamin Kallos

Carlyle Capital

"THEY'VE TAKEN THE BURDEN OF COMPUTER SUPPORT AND MAINTENANCE OFF MY BACK"

"Thanks to the Brainlink IT service, the entire burden of computer support is taken off my back, and I don't have to worry about security threats or downtime. Now we are getting regular Microsoft updates, virus updates, spyware is being scanned and removed, the temporary files are getting cleaned up, and our backups are being taken care of. It's really helped speed up our network, our programs run better, and we don't have the recurring problems that we had in the past.

For a small business like ours, Brainlink IT just makes sense. It gives you the real necessities of support you need at a very fair price. When you are running a business, you need to maintain a focus on keeping your clients happy and the income coming in. That takes precedence over removing temp files or scanning for spyware. But you can't ignore those things either or it will come back and develop into bigger problems. The support provided through the Brainlink IT takes that worry off my mind. It's really rare to find an IT support company that caters to the small business owner like me."

Andrew Weltchek, Esq.

WeltchekLaw.com

Commercial and Residential Real Estate Advisory Services

"BRAINLINK IMPROVED OUR CLIENT COMMUNICATIONS AND EVENT PLANNING, WHILE GIVING US A PREDICTABLE MONTHLY BILL"

Before we met Brainlink, we had ok IT service. What frustrated us was being charged by the hour. We never knew what our bill would be and the smallest of problems or simplest of questions generated at least two hours of billable time.

Raj & his team at Brainlink fixed our existing problems and made several cost-effective suggestions for improving our workflow, all while giving us a predictable monthly bill.

In addition, Brainlink spent three months learning about our business and then **helped us implement tools** to serve our clients better. Raj worked hand-in-hand with us to implement SendOutCards, Cardscan and InfusionSoft, **which improved our client communications and event planning.**

Raj is a great partner in not just IT, but in using technology to grow your business. I highly recommend him and Brainlink.

Erin Ardleigh

Wechsler Associates, Inc.

212-583-0800

eardleigh@wassociatesny.com

WE'RE SAVING SOMEWHERE BETWEEN $30,000 TO $40,000 A YEAR THANKS TO THE BRAINLINK'S IT SERVICE

My experience so far with Brainlink International, Inc. has been nothing but amazing; they have consistently gone above and beyond our expectations. The technician that works with us from Brainlink International, Inc. is one of the best engineers that I've ever worked with. He is forward thinking and plans out what we're going to need in the months and years to come instead of thinking only quick fix and short term. He's taken care of everything and it really has made my life a heck of a lot easier.

I would say that we are probably saving somewhere between $30,000 to $40,000 dollars a year thanks to Brainlink International, Inc. The capabilities they bring to the table are everything we were looking for. Plus, the fact that they monitor our network 24/7/365 takes a lot or responsibility off of everyone at the company, myself included.

They are dedicated, very professional and always available. There hasn't been one time that I have called Brainlink International, Inc. where I did get a prompt response. I've called him late in the evening and way early in the morning outside of normal business hours and they're always available and willing to help in whatever I need."

Kevin S. Daly

Insurance, Wealth Advisory and Financial Planning Services

"BRAINLINK ALLOWS US TO CONCENTRATE ON OUR CLIENTS, NOT OUR COMPUTERS"

"At OfficeLinks, we provide clients with a workplace environment where their business will thrive. Delivering next-generation, on-demand office space, video conference studios and meeting rooms requires enterprise-grade technology, seamless IT support and innovative tools. Brainlink allows us to concentrate on enabling our clients to open offices in premier locations including the Trump Tower (40 Wall Street, NY), 1440 Broadway (NY) and the Sears/Willis Tower in Chicago. Their Fixed-Fee IT Support is an exceptional product and provides significant value to our clients.

To me, it makes a lot of financial sense to pay a monthly fee to make sure our computer network is up and running than to have to pay thousands of dollars to fix a problem that could have been prevented in the first place. Knowing that the Brainlink team is watching over our data and the network gives me peace of mind that's priceless. It's almost like having your own personal IT team on staff—but without the overhead and costs."

Brainlink is a valued partner and we recommend them to our clients.

If you want the best in serviced office space, get it at The OfficeLinks.

If you want the best in fixed-fee IT, with great support, hire Brainlink."

> Harsh Mehta,
>
> Executive Vice President, The OfficeLinks.

"WE SWITCHED TO BRAINLINK'S FIXED MONTHLY FEE SYSTEM AND I COULDN'T BE HAPPIER WITH THE RESULT"

For many years, we had been using a different outside consultant but their hourly billing system was not transparent and we didn't feel like we were getting the service that we needed.

First, Raj and his team spent a lot of time analyzing our network before making recommendations. The thing that impressed me the most was that he brought in three different technicians—all with different specializations—to get our network updated and secured. I know that they put in a lot of time and effort to get everything up and running, but from our standpoint, it was seamless. They never got in our way and it didn't interrupt us here in the office.

We have the peace of mind that our network is being watched and properly maintained. Everyone here is very productive because issues are resolved quickly and painlessly—the flat monthly rate that we pay gives them an incentive to be very efficient and it really shows! I like the personal service Brainlink International, Inc. provides and the fact that I can pick up the phone or email them anytime with a question and get an answer right away. I genuinely get the feeling that Raj and the team at Brainlink International, Inc. want to help me, and that is, I think, the thing that I appreciate most."

Ms. Jackie Renton

Vice President, AION Partners

Property Management

CHAPTER 21

ABOUT RAJ GOEL

I am the Co-Founder and Chief Technology Officer (CTO) of Brainlink International, Inc., a technology company specializing in cutting-edge services and training to meet HIPAA, Sarbanes-Oxley, and Graham-Leach-Bailey security compliance requirements; in providing cyber forensic services for lawyers and accountants; as well as providing professional disaster recovery services, database development, CRM implementations, reporting and analytics for corporations and entrepreneurs.

I am a Certified Information Systems Security Professional (CISSP®) in good standing, and conducts HIPAA compliance reviews, re-mediation and training for hospitals and medical practices including Franklin Healthcare, Lowe Healthcare Worldwide, and the Rutland Regional Medical Center. I also conduct security compliance audits and re-mediation for corporate clients including the Rockland County Government (VT), and B&H Photo.

I am a cyber-forensics expert serving the needs of attorneys and forensic accountants. I conduct information security liability audits and IT valuations as well as tracking down and evaluating digital evidence. I am an experienced pre-trial consultant and expert witness in matrimonial proceedings, wrongful-termination suits, and in criminal defense matters.

I have over 20 years of experience in software development, systems integration, network communications, and eCommerce applications for the legal, financial, banking, insurance, real estate, healthcare, and pharmaceutical industries.

I have been a featured speaker at the New York State Society of CPAs, New York Health Information Management Association, New York State CyberSecurity Conference, InfoSecurity Toronto, Credit Interchange Association, New York County Lawyers' Association, and a host of other conferences. I have also been the featured presenter in Webinars for BrightTalk Security Summit ("Trends in Financial Crimes"), the ISC2 Security Series ("Staying Compliant in a Rapidly Changing World"), Citibank ("Are You Googling Your Privacy Away"), and other companies.

I have authored numerous articles, the most recent being: "Trends in Financial Crimes," and "Are You Googling Your Corporate Privacy and Security Away," for InfoSecurity Magazine, plus a monthly "Ask the Technologist" column for Commercial Property News.

In addition to starting my own company, I have served as Manager of Internet Services for Market Guide, Inc., where my team built the IP infrastructure; as the eBusiness re-architect for Schering-Plough, Inc., where we launched and managed Clarinex.com; and as the Global Information Security Officer for a major retailer.

I received a BS in Computer Science from the New York Institute of Technology, where I graduated Magna Cum Laude. I am a graduate of Landmark Education's Team Management and Leadership Program, a two-year training in leading and managing teams to produce outstanding results.

I am a member of the Information Systems Security Association; and serve on the technology board of the Association of Cancer Online Resources (ACOR.org).

ACCOUNT EXPERIENCE—By Type of Company

Pharmaceutical • Healthcare

Alice Peck Day Hospital (VT)

Association of Online Cancer
Resources (ACOR.org)

Brooklyn Bureau of Community
Services

Clarinex.com

Diabetes Learning Lab.com

ENT & Allergy Associates

Franklin Healthcare

Internet Health Coalition

Lowe Healthcare Worldwide (IPG)

Lowe Health Tech (IPG)

LIPIX

Rockingham County Govt. (NH)

Rutland Regional Medical Center
(VT)

Schering-Plough

Executive Suites • Office Business Centers

OfficeLinks

NYC Office Suites

World-Wide Business Centers

Finance • Insurance • Legal

Carnegie Associates Ltd.

Fuji Alternative Assets
Management Co.

Jeffrey L. Steinmann

John Hancock Mutual Life
Insurance Co.

Lichtenstein Financial Services

Nippon Credit Asset
Management Co.

Private Export Funding
Corporation (PEFCO)

Matrimonial Attorneys
(Details Upon Request)

Criminal Defense Cases
(Details Upon Request)

Wechsler Associates

Real Estate Services • Architects

AION Partners

Jeffrey Beers International

Real Data Management

RealNet.com

Manufacturing • Transportation • Logistics

American Auto Logistics (ASL Group)

Anthony Lawrence-Belfair

Exel Logistics

Halcraft, Inc.

H. Fox & Co.

Laird Technologies

RNK Distributing

Advertising • Media

Bingo.com

ConsumerSearch.com

eHarlequin.com

Harris Connect (social & mobile media platforms)

Hearst New Media

Interpublic Group (IPG)

iVillage.com

Lowe Healthcare Worldwide

Lowe HealthTech

The New York Times

Women.com

Haute Couture

Gabrielle Carlson Atelier

Additional Clients

B&H Photo

Brooklyn Bureau of Community Services

Internet Democracy Initiative (New York University)

United Federation of Teachers Technology Center

Chapter 22

Magazine Articles

Are you Googling Your Privacy Away?— InfoSecurity Magazine

Googling Security and Privacy

> The search giant saves a lot of information. Here's what you should know.

It's no secret that Google retains search data and metadata regarding searches—in fact, it's quite open about doing so. What's unsure, though, is the long-term threat to information security and privacy.

Let's review Google's elements.

Google Search: This search engine is gathering many types of information about online activities. Its future products will include data gathering and targeting as a primary business goal.

All of Google's properties—including Google Search, Gmail, Orkut and Google Desktop—have deeply linked cookies that will expire in 2038. Each of these cookies has a globally unique identifier (GUID) and can store search queries every time you search the Web. Google does not delete any information from these cookies.

Therefore, if a list of search terms is given, Google can produce a list of people who searched for that term, which is identified either by IP address or Google cookie value. Conversely, if an IP address or Google cookie value is given, Google can also produce a list of the terms searched by the user of that IP address or cookie value.

Orkut: Google's social-networking site contains confidential information such as name, email address, phone number, age, postal address, relationship status, number of children, religion and hobbies. In accordance with its terms of service, submitting, posting or displaying any information on or through the Orkut.com service automatically grants Orkut a worldwide, nonexclu-sive, sublicensable, transfer-able, royalty-free, perpetual, irrevocable right to copy, distribute, create derivative works of, and publicly perform and display such data.

Gmail: The primary risk in using Gmail lies in the fact that most users give their consent to make Gmail more than an email-delivery service and enable features such as searching, storage and shopping. This correla-tion of search and mail can lead to potential privacy risks. For example, email stored on third-party servers for more than 180 days is no longer protected by the Electronic Communications Privacy Act, which declares email a private means of communication.

Gmail Mobile: Mobile phones are increasingly being sold with Gmail built in, and if not, it can be down-loaded. The questions to ask: How uniquely does your mobile phone identify you as the user, and when was the last time you changed your phone and your identifiers?

Gmail Patents: Gmail's Patent #20040059712 emphasizes "Serving adver-tisements using information associated with email." This allows Google to create profiles based on a variety of information derived from emails related to senders, recipients, address books, subject-line texts, path name of attachments and so on.

Google Desktop: Google Desktop allows users to search their desktops using a Google-like interface. All word-based documents, spreadsheets, emails and images on a computer are instantly searchable. Index information is stored on the local computer. Google Desktop 3 allows users to search across multiple computers. GD3 stores index and copies of files on Google's servers for nearly a month.

Chrome: Chrome is Google's browser. It's available for download today and will eventually be installed on new PCs. Some of the risks it poses include:

• Every URL visited gets logged by Google

• Every word, partial word or phrase typed into the location bar, even if you don't click the Enter/Return button, gets logged by Google

• Chrome sends an automatic cookie with every automatic search it performs in the location bar.

Android: Android is Google's operating system for cell phones. It retains information about dialed phone numbers, received phone-call numbers, Web searches, emails and geographic locations at which the phone was used.

Google Health: This product allows consumers—

such as employees, coworkers and customers—to store their health records with Google. Recently, CVS Caremark, along with Walgreens and Longs Drugs in the United States, agreed to allow Google Health users to import their pharmacy records.

Organizational Threats

Uninstalling these products or using competitive tools can mitigate many of these threats. But what about the dangers to your organization? One example is Google Search with its Google Flu Trends (www.google.org/flutrends).

Google has correlated flu data from the U.S. Centers for Disease Control (CDC) from 2003 to the present with its own search data. Spikes in users' searches about flu treatments correlated tightly with the CDC data. Flu Trends has demonstrated Google's ability to analyze search data for a specific term or set of terms. And it can retain this data and where it came from

because Google in its privacy policies states that it records IP addresses.

So, what's to stop Google from analyzing all search data from your organization's networks? What's the difference between analyzing flu trends and "Top 100 search terms from XYZ Corp."? Or what if a company were to correlate regional threats from swine flu with search data from Google Health/Prescription data and then analyze the health of its employees and detect long-term effects?

Overall, the most critical threat is reliance on Gmail—whether the setting is universities, cities, companies or countries switching to Gmail en masse, or the newest employees in the organization using Gmail as their primary or sole email platform.

Questions to ask your security team: How big is the organization's email archive? How many years of emails are saved? If your organization switches its email hosting service to Google Gmail,

what happens to the privacy and confidentiality clauses in your employee and customer contracts?

Another area of concern for hosted email is the potential of having to turn that data over to the government. Google, Yahoo and Microsoft have a history of complying with the United States' and foreign governments' requests for information. If such data is turned over, how much corporate security is being eroded?

Consider the amount of money and manpower dedicated to handling Microsoft Windows patches, viruses, spyware and botnet detection. Imagine the impact that reliance on Google products could have on corporate privacy and security.

Raj Goel, CISSP, is chief technology officer of Brainlink International, an IT services firm. He is located in New York and can be reached at raj@goel.com.

TRENDS IN FINANCIAL CRIMES—*INFOSECURITY* MAGAZINE

MALICIOUS ATTACKS ON DATABASES and incidents of online and other tech-related thefts continue to evolve in number and manner—leaving both consumers and businesses scrambling to pay for the damage to their reputations and bottom lines. The Identity Theft Resource Center reports that in the first half of 2009, 18.4 percent of all breaches were from insider theft. That's up from 15 percent in 2008 and 6 percent in 2007. During the same period, the ITRC reports that hacking totaled 18 percent of all data breaches, compared with 11.7 percent in 2008. Combined, these malicious attacks are up more than 10 percent in 2009, with data breaches and insider theft accounting for 36 percent of the 250 reported breaches this year.

Information security experts, including ITRC, say companies must implement effective data-protection policies and

ITRC suggests any entity that requests personal information should have the technology and policies in place to limit access of sensitive information. For instance, companies can set up verification systems so that a consumer should not be asked for his or her Social Security number to view, for instance, a current balance.

GLOBAL SUPPLY CHAIN RISKS

Fake receipts and counterfeit gear are just a couple of examples of crimes that have swept through global supply chains. Fake receipts include everything from fake ticket stubs and railway passes sold online by unscrupulous companies to fake restaurant or taxi receipts turned in by unscrupulous employees looking to pad expenses.

One recent business scammer fraudulently raised $50 million from local investors by using fake receipts to support a lie about the number of existing U.S. customers signed on with his business. In another case, Chinese authorities reported seizing several warehouses

pant because so much of the information required to commit ID theft is available online due to inadequate controls, data leaks or human behavior.

For instance, ITRC reports that as of June 15, 2009, only 0.4 percent of all breaches involving laptops or other portable storage devices had encryption or other strong protection methods in use. Another 7.2 percent of reported breaches had data password protection. That leaves 92.4 percent of sensitive data with no protection at all. And ITRC reports that many of these breaches are

PROFESSIONAL,

High-tech professional criminals are getting ever more clever, says Raj Goel.

systems to safeguard their businesses and customers. Knowing what you are up against is a solid start in planning a defense against would-be thieves—from both inside and outside your company.

What follows are some of the latest trends in information security breaches and technology-related theft examples that hold valuable lessons for information security professionals.

IDENTIFICATION THEFT

Identification theft continues to run ram-

repeated events affecting the same company or agency.

PrivacyRights.org reports that between 2005 and 2009, companies reported losing more than 431 million data records, primarily those of U.S. citizens. Stolen personal information has, in turn, created a vast black market for hijacked credit card numbers and bank account credentials. As of April 2009, Symantec reports that hijacked credit card numbers were being sold for as little as 6 cents per card in lots of 10,000.

full of fake receipts worth an estimated $147.3 billion dollars.

Another booming criminal business is the production and sale of counterfeit technology. For instance, the U.S. Federal Bureau of Investigation recently discovered nearly $2 million in counterfeit Cisco Systems gear that leading private companies and leading government agencies were using unknowingly.

Government investigators and industry experts say the Cisco example highlights a need for companies' IP protec-

89

tion teams, resellers, law enforcement liaisons and customer service teams to stay in touch and be aware of red flags such as customer complaints.

ONLINE BANKING AND MORTGAGE FRAUD

Banks across the globe have spent billions of dollars over the past few years encouraging consumers to shift to online banking. And businesses everywhere

BEWARE!
Here are the latest trends in financial crimes.

have implemented more and more self-serve transaction methods—online and in person.

However, not all security ramifications have been thought out. For instance, if a customer logs into her bank account and a piece of malware transfers funds out of her account, who is liable?

In the U.S. home mortgage industry, meanwhile, reports

of criminals targeting owners of rental properties or second homes with attractive refinancing offers are on the rise. Using data supplied by the victims, the criminals forge credentials, refinance properties and abscond with the funds.

And when risky business practices in the subprime loan and mortgage market played out as a leading cause of the global financial meltdown, many people were surprised to find out just how many banks and lenders had inadequate internal digital controls.

In one sample case, a vocational nurse violated HIPAA's provisions and stole the identification of a 72-year-old woman. The nurse and three accomplices were able to cash out $165,000 of the woman's home equity.

SPAM, MALWARE AND INSECURE CODING

According to a new survey by the Messaging Anti-Abuse Working Group

(MAAWG), 12 percent of Internet users admitted clicking on spam because they were interested in the product or service offered. Eighty percent said they didn't believe they were at risk from malware when doing so.

And it's not just criminals who are peddling fake antivirus software or bogus spyware, or botnet herders hijacking machines. For instance, the New York attorney general's office in 2007 fined Priceline, Travelocity and Cingular for using adware programs to market their products.

Meanwhile, insecure or bad coding—whether it's a flaw in APIs from the same vendor that has acquired other companies or multiple companies agreeing on the same insecure standards or single-vendor flaws—is likely here to stay.

For instance, HIPAA is touted as a good first step in protecting the electronic storage of medical data, but it only applies to doctors, hospitals, insurance companies and the government. It excludes pharmaceutical companies and services to which consumers voluntarily give their health information. Industry watchers say new online health concerns, such as Google Health, Microsoft Health and other services that are exempt from HIPAA-required controls, will lead to further privacy erosions due to flaws in their APIs or third-party APIs.

THE BOTTOM LINE

The Ponemon Institute reports that in 2005, the cost for companies that lost 10,000 records or more was $138 per record to clean up. By 2008, the cost per lost record rose to $202. Multiply that by 10,000 records and it skyrockets to more than $2 million.

Security experts say the best defense is to learn from trends in crimes, and use the knowledge to revise and build better policies and systems in cooperation with industry peers and government agencies—because you will be targeted again. (ISC)²

Raj Goel, CISSP, is chief technology officer of Brainlink International, an IT services firm. He is located in New York and can be reached at raj@brainlink.com.

CREATING STRONG PASSWORDS—*ENTREPRENEUR* MAGAZINE

Power passwords

You know you shouldn't use sequential numbers, your birthdate or your child's name. But how do you come up with hack-resistant passwords that you can easily remember?

Raj Goel, founder of Brainlink International, an information technology security firm in New York City, has a series of tricks he uses to train executives in creating great passwords:

Pick a line from a song or a book title. Something you'll remember, but not something people immediately associate with you. For example, you might choose *The Power of Positive Thinking*, by Norman Vincent Peale.

Select the second, third or fourth letter from each word. Choosing the second letter would yield HOFOH. The third would be EWSI. Those are your base passwords. It's a good idea to have a few of them, he says.

Then, add numbers and special characters such as !, @, # in between the letters of the base password. Integrating the symbols for 1 through 6 into the base password would yield !H@O#F$O%H^. You could also use the symbols for a number that is meaningful to you, such as a former ZIP code backwards or a date that is not your birthday or anniversary. For websites, you can customize the password by integrating the name of or an identifying detail about the website, !H@O#eBayF$O%H^. Mixed-case passwords are stronger.

By having a variety of base passwords customized in ways that are easy for you to remember, you eliminate the need to keep a written list of passwords, which can be risky. Goel also suggests that you use different base passwords for different areas of your life. For example, one for work, another for banking and financial activities, still another for personal websites, such as shopping sites. —G.M.

BACKING UP DOCUMENTS IN THE CLOUD—LAW.COM

John Edwards did a great job of summarizing various backup tools available for CLOUD backups, and some risks inherent in it.

My opinion is that law firms should NOT be using public or hybrid clouds, as dangers to client-confidentiality and potential litigation liabilities outweigh any short-term savings.

PRIVACY

Rajesh Goel, chief technology officer at Brainlink International, a New York-based compliance security consulting firm, warns that storing data in the cloud could, under some circumstances, pose a privacy risk to client data. "If a firm is large enough and they have the financial and technical resources to build their own private cloud, then the advantages of cloud computing are compelling," he says. "For firms lured by the low cost/save money siren song of public and hybrid clouds, there's danger ahead."

Goel observes that while the Electronic Communications Privacy Act assures that e-mail has a 180-day right to privacy, information held in databases has zero days of privacy protection. "All online applications... can be classified as databases, under the strict definition of ECPA," Goel asserts.

Goel says that attorneys also need to be aware of another potential privacy threat. "The Patriot Act allows law enforcement to use National Security Letters to obtain information about individuals and companies from service providers," he says. "Most NSLs forbid the service provider from notifying their clients that they have released information to law enforcement, based on NSLs."

Goel adds that lawyers with clients in highly regulated areas, such as health care and financial services, also need to fully investigate their situation and privacy risk potential before sending files into the cloud.

Full Article is available at:
http://www.law.com/jsp/article.jsp?id=1202509461694&Backing_Up_Documents_in_the_Cloud&slreturn=1&hbxlogin=1

What Should Matrimonial Attorneys Know About Cyberforensics—NYCLA Newspaper

According to surveys of U.S. and U.K. matrimonial attorneys, more and more of them are asking (or requiring) their clients to disclose Facebook, Twitter, LinkedIn, and other social media credentials to the attorney start of the case. The retained counsel has no wish to be surprised in court, by finding out that his or her client said or posted things online that are detrimental to the case.[1]

As a Cyberforensics consultant, I ask the following questions when working with lawyers in order for my clients to get the best results possible when fighting matrimonial cases:

1. Does your client (the wife, husband or partner) have a legal right to the computer or smartphone? If the device is jointly owned, then we can image and analyze it. If the device is owned by the other person's employer, or is somehow construed as private property, then we do not have the legal right to analyze it, without a court order.

2. Has a PRESERVATION LETTER been issued to the opposing side?

3. Has either side retained an expert to acquire multiple copies of legally compliant forensics images? If both sides agree that the image is forensically sound, then both sides can invest resources in evidence analysis, not re-acquisition.

4. How many devices are owned by the couple? Computers, laptops, smartphones, etc.

5. Do they have any shared passwords to e-mail, online banking, Facebook, LinkedIn, etc? If yes, then we ask the attorney retaining us to determine (and advise us in writing) whether their client still has a legal right to those passwords, now that the divorce process has started.

6. What are we looking for? Financial records? Evidence of online romances? Deleted files and documents?

The best way to minimize forensics costs is to limit what we need to look for.

Every client has something to hide.

Guide your forensics investigator—frame the request as narrowly as possible. For example, "find me financial records" or "we suspect he's hiding funds offshore" or "she's got a shopping addiction" or "we suspect he's having an affair."

7. Has anyone used non-forensics software to try an undelete files or used a non-forensic computer technician to gather evidence? If so, then there's a possibility that the evidence is spoiled and cannot be used in court. Based on my experience, even when the evidence cannot be presented in court, it often results in negotiated settlements.

8. Is there any suspicion of child pornography (CP) on the device(s)? Under current Federal laws, if we encounter more than three items of CP, we are legally obligated to stop work and report it to the FBI, Secret Service and ICE. Unlike any other form of evidence, mere possession of CP by an attorney (or their consultants) is illegal under federal law[2],[3] and attorneys have been prosecuted for possessing CP while they were conducting research on behalf of their clients.

See the case of Attorney Leo Thomas Flynn at www.brunolaw.com/prosecutionserves-as-warning.html.

Below are several case studies that illustrate the above points:

1. In a case, the family kept using the shared computer(s) months after the divorce was filed. Analysis of the data revealed that the husband had lied to the wife, and his attorney, about what he did with the couple's sex tapes, which were on the shared computer. Since the entire family (husband, wife, children, guests, etc.) used the same user name and password to log in to the computer, it was forensically impossible to tell who created, modified or deleted files -- this evidence was considered polluted and could not be used in court. While this evidence could not be used in court, it assisted the wife's attorney in negotiating a favorable settlement.

2. In another case, the husband fled from his native country to the U.S. 18 months ago. The wife followed suit six months later. She brought the family laptop with her, and presented it to her U.S. attorney as evidence. Having established the dates of his departure, and her departure from their native country, we started the analysis. We located some financial records. We also found large stashes of

adult imagery from dating sites—both male and female dating profiles. The initial conclusion we drew was that the husband was having a homosexual affair, or was bisexual, due to the prevalence of both male and female dating profiles. Upon review, the wife rejected the analysis. The discrepancies in the dates of profiles led us to re-interview the wife, with counsel present. During this re-interview, we discovered that after the husband had fled, the wife's sister has used the laptop to engage in online dating for the intervening six months. Because the client allowed her sister to use the laptop for six months, and did not communicate this with the attorney, all digital evidence had to be thrown out, because it was spoiled.

Defending Against Cyber Evidence

When defending against cyber-evidence, determine the legality of the evidence. In most cases, the evidence was spoiled or may have been collected illegally. Determine the correctness of evidence—the data may have been collected legally—but was it collected and analyzed correctly?

In one case, the client was charged with 107 counts, based on the fact that he clicked on one link, and the popup downloaded 50 images on the hard drive. Analysis by the author was able to prove that these were the result of popups downloading multiple images per click, and should therefore be counted as one violation per popup or web page. In the end, the client was charged with five counts—a far cry from the initial 107.

Social Media and Cloud Evidence

While we cannot gather forensic evidence from cloud providers (Facebook, Gmail, Twitter, World-of-Warcraft (WOW), Farmville, etc.), in many cases, once references to these services have been located on the clients' hard drives, you can subpoena log files from these providers. Facebook, WOW, and EZ-pass are great places to acquire digital evidence.

Raj Goel is founder and CTO of Brainlink International, Inc.

Learn more at www.RajGoel.com andwww.Brainlink.com.

References

1. www.guardian.co.uk/technology/2011/mar/-08/facebook-us-divorces, http://www.dailymail.co.uk/femail/article-2080398/Facebook-cited-THIRD-divorces.html, http://kotaku.com/5576262/farmville-world-of-warcraft-are-divorce-lawyers-latest-weapons-in-court

2. www.orangecountycriminaldefenselawyerblog.com/2011/02/in-orange-county-ca-whathappe.html

3. www.brunolaw.com/prosecution-serves-as-warning.html

Chapter 23

How Does Your Current Computer Guy Stack-up?

The good news about computers is that they do what you tell them to do. The bad news is that they do what you tell them to do.

TED NELSON

Take this quiz and find out!

How can you tell if you're receiving poor or substandard service? How do you know if your computer guy is doing everything possible to protect your business from downtime, viruses, data loss or other disasters? Could your current computer technician actually be jeopardizing your network?

If your technician does not score a "yes" on every point, you are (probably) paying for substandard support.

- ❏ Do they respond to emergencies in 1 hour or less?
- ❏ Are they easy to reach and responsive when you need them for non-emergencies?
- ❏ Do they offer an ongoing maintenance program to keep critical security settings and patches up-to-date?
- ❏ Do they offer a monitoring system to watch over your network 24/7/365 for developing problems?
- ❏ Do they proactively offer new ways to improve your network's performance, or do they wait until you have a problem before making recommendations?
- ❏ Do they provide detailed invoices that clearly explain what you are paying for?

- ❏ Do they explain what they are doing and answer your questions in terms that you can understand?
- ❏ Did they complete projects on time?
- ❏ Do they follow up on your requests quickly?
- ❏ Do they offer any guarantees on their services?
- ❏ Do they arrive on time and dress professionally?
- ❏ Do they have other people on staff familiar with your network in case your regular technician goes on vacation or gets sick?
- ❏ Do their technicians participate in ongoing training?
- ❏ Do they listen to you?
- ❏ Are they adamant about backing up your network and having a disaster recovery plan in place?
- ❏ Do they understand the laws and regulations that apply to your business?
- ❏ Are they committed to helping your business grow?

CHAPTER 24

THANK YOU

Money is not the most important thing.
But it's right up there with oxygen.

ROBIN ROBINS

It has been my honor and privilege to share with you, ideas and techniques that help our clients grow.

I know it's not an easy task selecting an IT partner—it's like choosing a new lawyer or a new CPA. You will only want to do it if you lose faith in your current vendor.

It is my hope that you, and every other small business owner, uses technology as a competitive advantage to grow your business, reduce costs, increase your profitability, and take care of your families.

Our mission at Brainlink has always been very simple:

Our mission is to help your business become MORE profitable.
Our goal is to offer excellent service so that you will have no reservations about referring others to us who have similar needs as yours.

Thank you for taking the time to read this book.

If you have any questions about IT, this book, or any other related issues, please email me at raj@brainlink.com or call me at 917-685-7731.

Resources & Recommendations

Networking Groups

I strongly recommend that you join a professional networking group for business, rather than a fraternity or social networking group.

BNI—Business Network International—www.bni.com

If you've not networked before, this is the place to begin. Dr. Ivan Misner has created a system that trains beginners and experts alike, in the art of business networking. BNI has chapters in every major city in the world.

Gotham City Networking, Inc—www.gothamnetworking.com

Gotham is for experienced networkers—if you know how to network, play well with others, and have a great follow up system, Gotham IS the place to be. However, if you've not networked before, spend at least 1-2 years learning how to network, before you dive into Gotham.

Gotham exists primarily in NYC, Nassau County, Suffolk County, Connecticut, Boston, Princeton and Miami – so, if you ARE an experienced networker and there's a Gotham chapter nearby, why not join up!

Books

The 4-Hour Workweek, Timothy Ferriss, www.fourhourworkweek.com

> To say that this book is a life-changer is an understatement. The biggest mistake most entrepreneurs make is not learning how to delegate. In this book, Tim demonstrates a number of small and large ways to delegate tasks to others. If you can learn how to do this,

THE MOST IMPORTANT SECRETS TO GETTING GREAT RESULTS FROM I T

you can shorten your workweek substantially. Tim's book opened my eyes to a whole universe of delegating.

This book is living proof of the lessons I learned from Tim Ferriss.

Yes, I wrote the manuscript. But I delegated other things.

Carolynl from Fiverr.com did the proof reading.

Blaine from Vervante did the cover design

My friends and family critiqued the book design.

If I'd tried to do it all myself, completing this book would have been impossible.

Get Things Done, David Allen, www.davidco.com

The reason most of us don't delegate is because just trying to manage tasks, promises and deliverables is a real challenge for ourselves. Trying to also manage your assistants, co-workers, etc is even more daunting. I find that the GTD philosophy works – for me, and for some of my clients. If you do nothing else, read the first 2 chapters of GTD and see if this simple workflow doesn't help to make your life easier.

See http://lifedev.net/2007/02/gtd-cheatsheet-the-workflow/

Getting Control of Your Life: The Five Stages of Mastering Workflow - http://www.wikisummaries.org/Getting_Things_Done:_The_Art_of_Stress-Free_Productivity -

The Greatest Salesmen In The World, Og Mandino

I found this book very useful. I have no idea why book stores put this in the section on religion—it's better than most self-help books AND it's an easy read.

Never Eat Alone, Keith Ferrazzi, www.keithferrazzi.com

If you're going to network (see BNI and Gotham above), then you might as well do it right. This book lays out a tactical plan for getting the most out of your networking, conferences, travel, etc.

Steven Lichtenstein recommended this book to me 6 years ago…and I still re-read it annually and get new insights with each re-reading.

The Landmark Forum, www.landmarkeducation.com

I am a graduate of the Landmark Curriculum for Living, The Communications Program and the Team Management & Leadership programs.

It's impossible to calculate the tremendous value that participating in Landmark has had on all aspects of my life; from marriage and parenting to business and play.

I credit the Landmark Forum for eliminating stress from my life.

The SELP helped me convert a long-time competitor into a business partner.

The Communications weekends improved my marriage and my relationships with clients.

The promise of the Team Management & Leadership 1 (TMLP-2) course is that you can learn to run a small company. The promise of TMLP-2 is that you can learn to run a small country.

Taking the TMLP-1 course helped my company in many ways. Although business was still a struggle, we were improving and growing our revenues.

TMLP-2 set us squarely on the road to profitability. I learned to delegate at a global level, learned how to make clear, concise requests, and how to deliver at unprecedented levels.

I don't get a penny, or a toaster, when you complete the Forum. However, your life will change dramatically. Why not join and find out what it can mean for you too?

Highly recommended.

OFFERS FOR YOU

It is better to give, than to receive. But what goes around, comes around.

FRED KLEIN

Dear Reader,

Thanks for sticking with me so far. Our mutual journey has just started…but it's far from over.

1. **Drinks at the Friars Club (www.friarsclub.com)**

   Should you find yourself in NYC, and would like to be my guest at the Friars, then please give me a call. I'm always delighted to take old clients, or new friends and acquaintances to the Friars.

2. **Be my guest at Gotham Networking (www.gothamnetworking.com)**

   On any given weekday, there's a Gotham event going on. If you'd like to check out the magic of Gotham, meet some great people, and create long-lasting relationships, come as my guest to a future Gotham Meeting.

3. **Invite me to speak at your next meeting or event**

   If you like what you read in this book, or what you've seen at my presentations and webinars at www.RajGoel.com, then please invite me to speak at your next event. I'm happy to speak at Corporate meetings, Bar Associations, Accounting Societies, CLE events, CPE events, etc.

4. **Build a great Follow Up System**

   If you have a pile of business cards, and you need a better way to manage them, check out www.BusinessCardMastery.com. Mention this book and get 50% off.

Stay Happy, Healthy & Secure!

—Raj